HOW TO USE THIS BOOK

CHECK OUT THE VIDEOS! Please notice the plural **videos**. This single workbook corresponds to three of our Video Course Reviews: *The Wild and Wacky World of Finance* Parts 1, 2, and 3. You'll be much better off if you buy and watch all three tapes.

FOLLOW ALONG. The **VIDEO NOTES** section does your work for you! We've already taken all of your notes—all you have to do is follow along with the videos. We've even given you a **VIDEO TIME CODE** for both videos. Just reset your VCR counter to 0:00:00 when the Cerebellum logo appears at the beginning of each tape. These clocks 0:00:00 give you the time code for each important section so you know where to fast-forward to! This will enable you to learn and retain material much more effectively. Just stop the tape after a difficult section and read through your notes!

Also, so you'll know which video we're talking about, we've put these markers in the upper right-hand corner: **V1**, **V2** and **V3**. **V1** means you're in a section that covers material from *The Wild and Wacky World of Finance Part 1*. **V2** means you're in a section that covers material from *The Wild and*

Wacky World of Finance Part 2, and **V3** means you're in a section that covers material from *The Wild and Wacky World of Finance Part 3.*

LEARN NEW STUFF. Unfortunately, we just can't include everything about finance in three videos. The **OTHER IMPORTANT STUFF** section gives other cool facts you'll need to ace your tests.

TEST YOURSELF. **QUIZZES** and **PRACTICE EXAMS** allow you to test yourself and make sure you've covered all the bases. The answers appear at the back—*don't cheat!*

HAVE FUN. The book is chock-full of diversions and stress relievers, and there are two neat flippy pictures at the bottom of each page.

THE STANDARD DEVIANTS™ STUDY SIDEKICK

THE WILD AND WACKY WORLD OF FINANCE PARTS 1,2, & 3 STUDY SIDEKICK (1ST EDITION)

Written by The Standard Deviants® Academic Team, including:
Gabrielle Smith
Mark Eppli, Ph.D.
Igor Torgeson

Edited by:
Rachel Galvin

Graphic Design by:
C. Christopher Stevens

800–238–9669
e-mail: cerebellum@mindspring.com
www.cerebellum.com

THE STANDARD DEVIANTS

OTHER SUBJECTS FROM CEREBELLUM:

- **Accounting**
- **Microeconomics**
- **Statistics**
- **Biology**
- **Physics**
- **Basic Math**
- **Trigonometry 1 & 2**
- **Geology**
- **Psychology**
- **Astronomy**
- **Pre-Calculus 1 & 2**
- **Calculus 1 & 2**
- **Chemistry 1, 2, & 3**
- **Algebra 1 & 2**
- **Organic Chemistry 1, 2, & 3**

For an updated list of titles available, check our web site.

www.cerebellum.com

Printed in the beautiful U.S.A.

TABLE OF CONTENTS

VIDEO TIME CODES

VIDEO NOTES

THE
STANDARD
DEVIANTS

Table of Contents

STUDY SIDEKICK

TEST YOURSELF

VIDEO NOTES

Table of Contents

THE
STANDARD
DEVIANTS

Table of Contents

STRESS RELIEF

ANSWERS

Table of Contents

VIDEO TIME CODE

The Wild and Wacky World of Finance Part 1

0:03:05 ....**I. Introduction**

0:03:20 ....A. Finance in the marketplace

0:03:30 ....1. Role of the financial manager

0:03:43 ....2. Types of businesses

a. Sole proprietorship

b. General and limited partnerships

c. Corporations

0:07:36 ....3. Double taxation

a. Example with double taxation

b. Example without double taxation

0:09:20 ....4. Corporation pros and cons

0:09:55 ....5. Goal of the financial manager

a. Maximizing stockholder wealth

b. Earnings per share

0:12:42 ....6. Dividend policy

0:13:55 ....7. Corporation structure

8. Agency problems 0:15:01
    a. Stockholder/manager
    b. Stockholder/bondholder

B. Different kinds of markets 0:19:25
1. Primary/secondary 0:19:55
2. Credit markets 0:20:36
3. Mortgage markets 0:20:45
4. Financial asset markets 0:20:52
5. Extra stuff 0:21:16

C. Financial statements 0:21:32
1. T-account 0:21:48
2. The annual report 0:22:34
    a. Balance sheet
        i. Assets and liabilities
        ii. Varieties of stock
    b. Income statement

D. Interest rates and yield curves 0:28:35
1. Real rate 0:29:28
2. Inflation premium 0:30:02
3. Treasury securities 0:30:45
4. Risk premium 0:31:04

0:31:31 ....5. Term structures of interest rates

a. Yield curve

b. Examples

0:36:00 ...**II. Time value of money**

0:36:48 ....A. Future value

0:37:16 ....1. Definition

a. Savings example

b. Debt example

0:39:39 ....2. Compounding: The long way

0:40:50 ....3. Compounding: The not-so-long way

0:43:27 ....4. Compounding: The short way

0:48:05 ....B. Future value of an annuity

0:48:16 ....1. What is an annuity?

0:51:12 ....2. Calculating annuities the long way

0:52:12 ....3. Annuities with the FVIFA

0:52:40 ....4. Annuity due

0:54:40 ....C. Present value

0:54:50 ....1. What is it?

0:55:55 ....2. PVIF

0:56:36 ....3. Example

0:57:57 ....4. Opportunity cost rate

Topic	Time code
D. Present value of an annuity due	0:58:25
1. PVIFA	0:58:50
2. Example	0:59:00
3. PV of an annuity due	1:00:31
E. Perpetuities	1:02:34
F. Different interest rates	1:05:53
1. Nominal rate	1:06:18
2. APR	1:06:48
3. EAR	1:07:25
G. Compounding: The master formula	1:09:26
H. Other important concepts	1:12:00
III. Basic financial concepts	1:14:21
A. Risk	1:14:30
B. Probability and rate of return	1:16:10
1. Probability	1:16:10
2. Rate of return	1:17:17
C. Risk and standard deviation	1:23:05
1. Standard deviation	1:23:16
2. Coefficient of variation	1:28:30

VIDEO NOTES

The Wild and Wacky World of Finance Part 1

0:03:05

Introduction

0:03:20

Section A: Finance in the Marketplace

Financial management is the key to the success of a business. It consists of obtaining and using funds to maximize the overall worth of the business.

Types of Businesses

Three different forms of businesses exist in the marketplace:

- ¢ The **sole proprietorship**
- ¢ The **partnership**
- ¢ The **corporation**

When determining which formation is best, potential business owners face two main concerns: taxes and personal liability. (They may also have also have personal concerns, such as a lack of confidence or a fear of buildings, but these play only a marginal role when selecting a business formation.)

VIDEO NOTES

A typical **sole proprietorship:**

- ¢ Is a business owned by one person.
- ¢ Is not considered a taxable entity.
- ¢ Has no taxes levied against the company itself; instead, taxes are levied on the personal income of the owner.

A **partnership:**

- ¢ Is a business that two or more people own without incorporating.
- ¢ Is easy to form.
- ¢ Has the same tax arrangement as the sole proprietorship, since it is not a separate, taxable entity.

There are two main types of partnerships: general and limited.

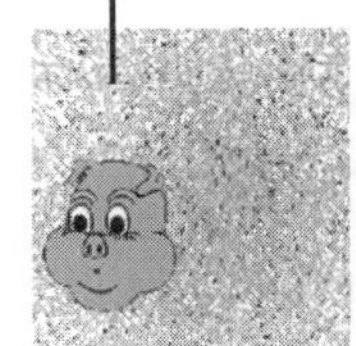

A **general partnership** exists when each partner is involved in the day-to-day management of the business and has unlimited liability for the debts incurred by the company.

Limited partnerships differ from general partnerships in that most limited partnerships are made up of a limited partner who supplies the money needed for the business, and a general partner who supplies the business expertise. Limited partners are held liable only up to their amount of investment in the business, but limited partners have no power in the day-to-day management of the business. The general partner has unlimited liability and all of the management power.

(Note: There are other forms of partnership such as the **One Guy Does All The Work And Other Guy Plays Video Games Partnership** or the **Two People On A Raft Deciding Which One To Eat First Partnership**, but only in rare situations do these apply to finance.)

Sole proprietorships and partnerships have two main advantages:

- ¢ Both are easy to form.
- ¢ Neither pay taxes at the entity level.

However, the sole proprietorship and the partnership also have three major disadvantages:

- ¢ Raising the necessary capital to start these types of businesses is difficult.
- ¢ Owners are personally liable for all of the business's debts.

VIDEO NOTES

- Businesses exist only as long as their owners do, so if the owner dies, the business dies too.

The third type of business formation is the **corporation**. The corporation, is a form of business that was created by a legislative act of the government. The corporation is a separate legal body that exists for the explicit purpose of conducting business. The owners of a corporation are called shareholders or stockholders. The size of an individual's ownership depends on how many shares of stock he or she holds. A corporation carries many of the same societal responsibilities that an individual does. For instance, it can sue and/or be sued, and it is taxed by Uncle Sam just like an individual.

The corporation has three main advantages:

- Investors are not personally liable for the actions or debts of the company. Although the corporation can be sued as a separate entity, its individual investors cannot be.
- Shifting ownership is easy. Ownership of a corporation can be divided into stock and sold in public markets.
- The corporation lives on even after its owners die.

Corporations have two main disadvantages:

- They are more complicated to form.
- They are taxed separately by the government. The **corporate income tax** yields double taxation because the business gets taxed as a separate entity, and then the **dividends** that the owners of the business receive get taxed as personal income.

(Many owners, enraged by the second disadvantage, have journeyed to Boston in protest and thrown countless sacks of tea into the harbor. Sadly enough, the rules have remained the same.)

Let's walk you through an example of the double taxation that corporations unfortunately face. Tattoo U Incorporated is a national chain of tattoo parlors featuring excellent and courteous service, a sterile environment, and the latest designs in tattoo formal wear.

For argument's sake, let's say that Tattoo U was a big hit this year. It had a taxable income of $600,000. Let's also assume that the marginal corporate income tax rate for this year is 38%. (Finance people call taxes "marginal" to combine state and federal and everything else, so we do it too. Don't freak.) So 38% of Tattoo U's income is paid to Uncle Sam. The shareholders own the corporation, and receive a financial return on their investment as dividends. But this is where the double taxation comes in. Once those dividend payments are sent to the shareholders, the government treats the payments as the personal income of each shareholder and taxes it again.

So the separate, corporate, legal entity of Tattoo U is taxed, and then its individual owners are taxed, too.

This contrasts with Our Heavenly Tattoo, a local tattoo parlor that is a sole proprietorship run and owned by Big Jimbo Floyd. Big Jimbo's income from Our Heavenly Tattoo is considered his

personal income, because his business is a sole proprietorship. So the income from the business is added to Big Jimbo's income without a separate tax on Our Heavenly Tattoo. Jimbo is taxed at his individual income tax rate—he's taxed only once.

Goal of the Financial Manager

Regardless of the form a business takes, the **financial manager** plays an important role in the success of the business. **The goal of the financial manager is to maximize stockholder wealth.** This goal must be at the forefront of all decisions the financial manager makes. The financial manager wants to maximize the cash flow and the stock appreciation of the business, while minimizing the risk that the business incurs.

One of the factors that the financial manager deals with the most is the **earnings per share** of the company's stock. Earnings per share equals the revenues of the corporation divided by the number of outstanding shares of stock.

$$\text{Earnings per share} = \frac{\text{Revenues of the corporation}}{\text{\# of outstanding shares of stock}}$$

The financial manager pays attention to the earnings per share because it is very important in the determination of stock price. Generally, the greater the expected cash flow coming into the business, the greater the earnings per share, and therefore, the greater the value of the stock.

My vocabulary sucks.
— C. Alan Canant

The one thing a financial manager shouldn't do is create risk for the company. **Risk** is the chance that what we expect to happen really won't happen. Stockholders expect to make money. The financial manager must monitor the cash flows, increase earnings, and reduce risk.

Although the financial manager is critical to a corporation's success, the manager's day-to-day decisions do not control the stock price (if the manager did have control over the stock price, the manager would be omnipotent and indispensible, allowing him or her to demand a bigger office and the shareholders' firstborn sons). Market perceptions or expectations determine the actual price of a corporation's stock.

A stock's market price is determined and affected by these factors, among others:

¢ Perceived ability to generate profit over time.

¢ Projected earnings per share of stock.

¢ Amount of future risk.

¢ Amount of corporate debt.

¢ The corporation's dividend policy.

Dividend Policy

Another responsibility of the financial manager is to create and maintain an appropriate **dividend policy**.

When a corporation makes money, the money is either sent to the shareholders through cash distributions called dividends, or retained by the corporation for investment in new projects and machinery. Shareholders, of course, enjoy receiving dividends. However, only by reinvesting some of its earnings can a business grow and consequently increase its stock value. The financial manager is responsible for managing dividend policy so that the shareholders are happy and the business can expand. If you ever grow up to be a financial manager, remember this one rule of thumb: "A good shareholder is a satisfied shareholder, and a bad shareholder is a shareholder who has to donate blood to buy toothpaste." **Happy managing!!!**

Corporate Structure

The financial manager, although in a very powerful position, does have to report to the chief executive officer (CEO) and the board of directors of the corporation. The board of directors is responsible to the shareholders at large.

The **president**, or chief executive officer, or CEO, is the person in charge of managing the corporation and reporting to the board of directors. Although the president runs the company, the board of directors is still in charge.

The **chief financial officer**, or CFO, is in charge of all financial management of the company, which includes both the treasury and the comptroller departments. The CFO usually reports to the CEO, and is frequently on the board of directors. The

treasury deals with cash flows, credit, or big investments (like acquisitions or purchases of new equipment and securities). The **comptroller** does more of the hands-on financial work, like accounting, payroll, and taxes.

The **vice presidents of production and sales** are at the same level as the CFO. They deal with production and sales. Surprising, isn't it.

Keep in mind that all of this can differ from company to company. What we've given you here is the basic and most accepted set-up.

For a more in-depth discussion, contact a local corporation and follow the CEO about town. Granted, this may be a difficult task, because most CEOs are "men on the move."

Agency Problems

Unfortunately, managers are not always working in the best interest of the corporation. The conflicts of interest that occur when managers put their own interest ahead of the interest of the corporation are referred to as **agency problems**. Agency problems occur when maximizing shareholder wealth fails to be the principal goal of a business.

There are two main types of agency problems:

stockholder-manager and **stockholder-bondholder.**

Video Notes

Stockholder-manager problems include conflicts between the interest of the stockholders, or owners, and the managers who run the company's operations. These problems often occur when management focuses more on its own wealth than on the stockholders' earnings.

There are at least four options for solving stockholder-manager problems:

- Offer stock incentives to the managers as a reward for achieving particular goals.
- Threaten to fire the management.
- A **proxy fight**: stockholders vote the management out of office.
- The threat of **hostile takeover**.

STUDY SIDEKICK

Stockholder-bondholder problems occur when there is tension between stockholders, who receive rewards for when the company takes risks, and bondholders, who do not benefit from risk. While stockholders may be willing to take risks in hopes of increased dividends, bondholders typically dislike risk because it decreases the value of their bonds.

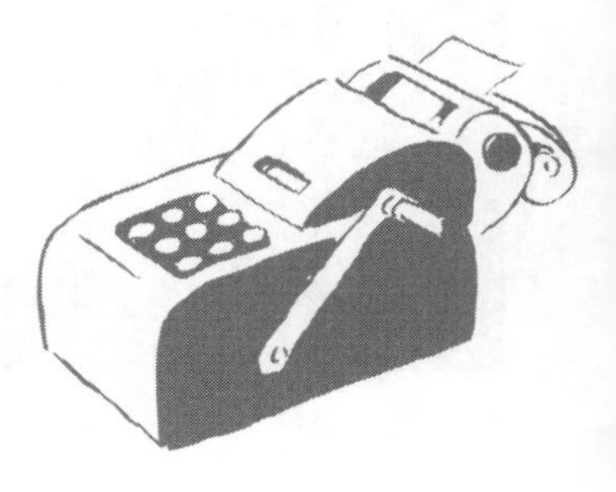

0:19:25

Section B: Different Kinds of Markets

A market is essentially any place where money, goods, or services are exchanged. In finance, we are primarily concerned with markets where money is invested. There are several types of investment markets.

$ **Money markets** are markets in which money is borrowed for less than one year.

$ **Capital markets** are markets in which securities lasting over one year in maturity are traded.

$ **Primary markets** are the markets in which "new" securities are sold (i.e., brand-new stocks sold directly from company to buyer).

$ **Secondary markets** are the markets in which "used" securities are sold. "Used" securities are stocks being traded not directly from the company but between investors—like on the New York Stock Exchange. Virtually all shares are purchased and sold on secondary markets.

$ Credit markets deal with short-term loans that involve relatively small amounts of money (like the kind you take to pay for school, cars, and wedding rings).

$ Mortgage markets deal in loans that use real estate as collateral.

$ Financial asset markets deal in stocks and bonds.

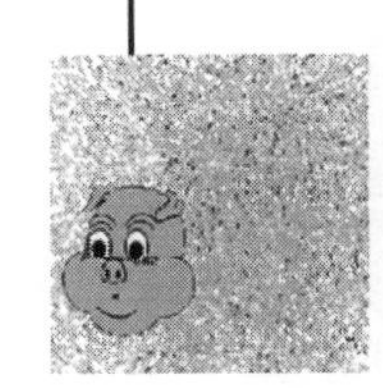

0:21:32

Section C: Financial Statements

The T-account and Accounting Equation

Financial statements illustrate the essence of a company's financial standing. Nearly all financial statements are based on the T-account. The **T-account** is a basic **accounting equation** which states that *assets are equal to liabilities plus capital or owners' equity.*

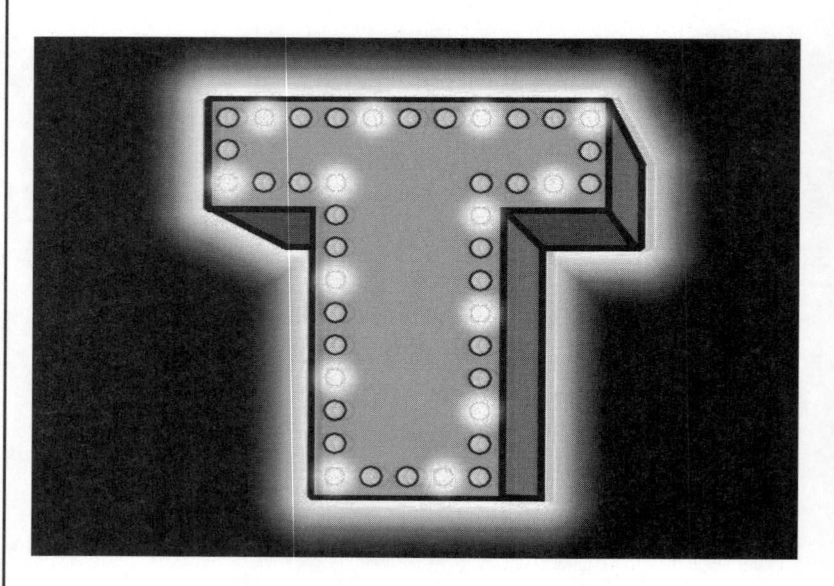

Assets are all the chunks of property that the company actually owns.

Liabilities are all the things the company owes to someone else, including the money it owes to bondholders.

Equity and **capital** are pretty much the same thing—either the money that the company has sitting around waiting to be invested, or the amount of money stockholders have invested in the company.

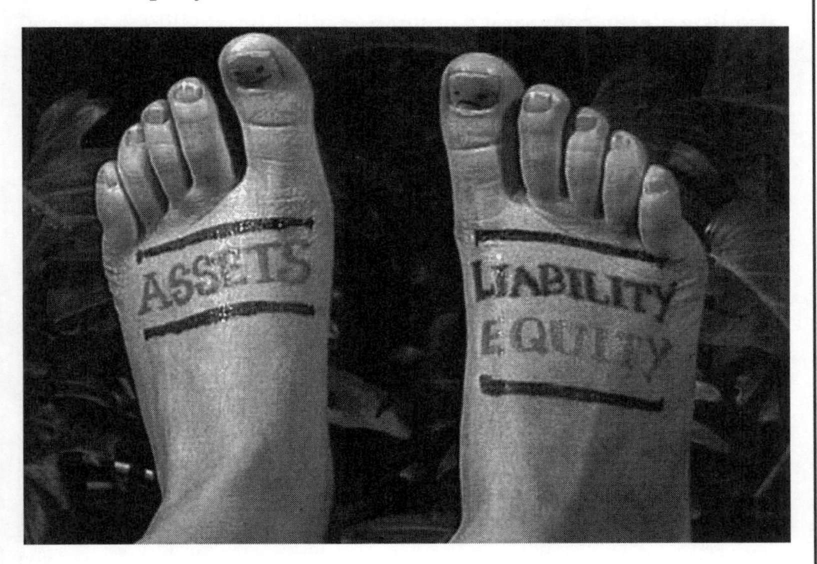

The Annual Report

The **annual report** is the most important financial statement that companies produce. The financial manager prepares the annual report for the company's shareholders and any other individuals interested in the business's financial performance. This report includes all of the company's yearly financial information, the officers' commentary on the year's results, and projected future earnings. Although the annual report does contain a **statement of cash flows** and a **statement of retained earnings**, its two most important components are the **balance sheet** and the **income statement**.

I think you got'er shut, chief.
— Igor

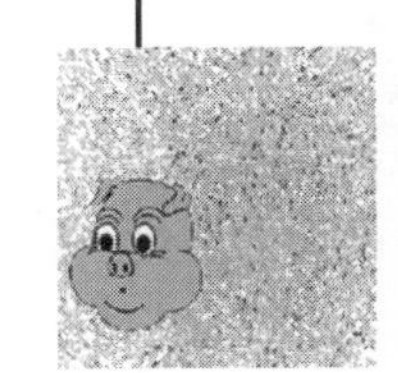

STUDY SIDEKICK

A **balance sheet** is a glimpse of a company's financial position at a certain point in time. The balance sheet lists all the company's assets (things of value), like cash on hand, inventory, accounts receivable, plants, and equipment. The balance sheet also lists all the company's obligations (liabilities), like accounts payable, stock, and **retained earnings**.

Naked Trampolining is cashing in on the wave of trampolining crossing the United States, and adding a new twist to this unusual sport: baby oil.

For Naked Trampolining, Inc., we see that it has total assets of $100,000, and total liabilities and equity of $100,000, because liabilities and equity must equal assets.

Balance Sheet for Naked Trampolining

December 31, 1996

ASSETS

Cash	$10,000
Inventory	$40,000
Accounts Receivable	$10,000
Plant and Equipment	$40,000
Total Assets	***$100,000***

LIABILITIES

Accounts Payable	$15,000
Other Liabilities	$10,000
Total Liabilities	***$25,000***

EQUITY

Stock	$50,000
Retained Earnings	$25,000
Total Equity	***$75,000***
Total Liabilities and Equity	***$100,000***

Study Sidekick

When studying a balance sheet, you will notice it lists two different classifications of stock: preferred and common.

Common stock represents a piece of ownership of a business, and brings with it the right to vote in the election of the board of directors. Common stockholders also receive dividends, but those dividends fluctuate based on the success or failure of the business.

Preferred stock, on the other hand, is a hybrid of bonds and common stock. Preferred stockholders do not have voting rights, but their dividends are fixed and do not fluctuate. Preferred stockholders receive the same dividend every period for as long as they hold the stock. However, a corporation's failure to make payment on preferred stock does not force it into **bankruptcy**, unlike failure to make payment on bonds.

The net worth of the company is also known as the **common stockholder's equity**. In an accounting sense, common stockholders' equity equals assets, minus liabilities, minus preferred stock.

STANDARD DEVIANT FINANCIAL INFO:

Typically, any preferred dividend shortfalls must be made up before any new dividends can be paid to common stockholders.

The **income statement** is also included in a corporation's annual report and helps investors evaluate the financial performance of the business. An income statement reviews a company's income and expenses or earnings for one year.

After the operating expenses comes another tricky expense, **depreciation**. Depreciation represents the wear and tear on a company's equipment, which causes it to fall in value over time. So while the company may have machines that it bought for $50,000, the machines may be worth only $45,000.

The government taxes a company on its income, but the wear and tear on the equipment reduces income. So we estimate a value of depreciation which reduces the amount of income subject to taxes. After we calculate income taxes, we add the depreciation back to the net income, because it's just a loss on paper, not an actual cash loss.

Although the balance sheet and the income statement are the statements referred to most frequently, a company's annual report also includes a statement of cash flow and a statement of retained earnings.

Here is a sample income statement.

Income Statement for Naked Trampolining

Gross Income	$10,000,000.00
Expenses	7,000,000.00
Depreciation	1,000,000.00
EBIT, Earnings Before Interest and Taxes	***2,000,000.00***
Interest	1,000,000.00
EBT, Earnings Before Taxes	***1,000,000.00***
Taxes (@35%)	350,000.00
NI, Net Income	***650,000.00***
Add back depreciation	1,000,000.00
NCF, Net Cash Flow	***1,650,000.00***

Section D: Interest Rates and Yield Curves

0:28:35

Interest rates are made up of several components. The symbol **K** is used to stand for the quoted market rate of interest or expected **rate of return**. This **quoted rate** is determined by combining three components: the **real rate**, the **inflation premium**, and the **risk premium**.

The Real Rate

The **real rate**, symbolized by **K***, is the rate on a riskless security, not including inflation. The real rate does not exist in the real world (which is kinda counterintuitive, huh?) because all securities include an inflation premium. The real rate is the first building block of all interest rates.

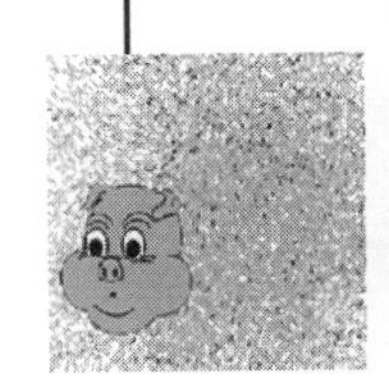

The Inflation Premium

The second component is the **inflation premium (IP)**. Because prices continually rise over time, an extra premium is added to the interest rate to account for inflation. Therefore, the inflation premium is added to the real rate to account for expected inflation over an entire lending period.

STANDARD DEVIANT FINANCIAL INFO:

Strictly speaking, you can't actually see the real rate in the real world, because all securities include a premium to compensate for the effects of inflation. However, recently the U.S. Treasury has begun issuing inflation-indexed bonds that can come close to approximating the real rate by adjusting the par value according to changes in inflation.

Risk Premium

The third component of interest rates is the **risk premium (RP)**. The risk premium is added to compensate for the risk of investing in a corporation. Variations in the RP are based on the per-

ceived riskiness of the corporation. For instance, a risky company has a high risk premium, and thus a high interest rate. (A *really* risky company would have a high risk premium and a dangerous, slippery walkway.)

Treasury Securities

An important term to understand when working with interest rates is **risk-free rate**. The risk-free rate is calculated by combining the real rate of return and the inflation premium.
For practical use, the interest rate on U.S. Treasury securities represents the risk-free rate because the government is considered free of risk. The symbol used to represent the risk-free rate is $\mathbf{K_{rf}}$.

Because U.S. Treasury securities represent the risk-free rate and therefore are referred to frequently by financiers, it is important to understand the different types of Treasury securities available.

There are essentially three types of Treasury securities available:

I just saw him this weekend. He's not that cool.
— Jennie Halfant

- **The T-bill**: Is a U.S. debt security that matures less than one year after it is issued.
- **The T-note**: Reaches maturity between one and ten years.
- **The T-bond**: Takes more than ten years to mature.

SUMMARY

- **Interest rates on corporate bonds are composed of the real rate of return, the inflation premium, and the risk premium.**
- **These all add up to the quoted interest rate for a given bond.**
- **The only investments without a risk premium are Treasury securities, because they are guaranteed by the full faith and credit of the U.S. government.**

Term Structure of Interest Rates

Another important concept in the discussion of interest rates is the relationship between short-term and long-term interest rates. This relationship is called the **term structure of interest rates**. History illustrates that long-term rates are typically greater than short-term rates.

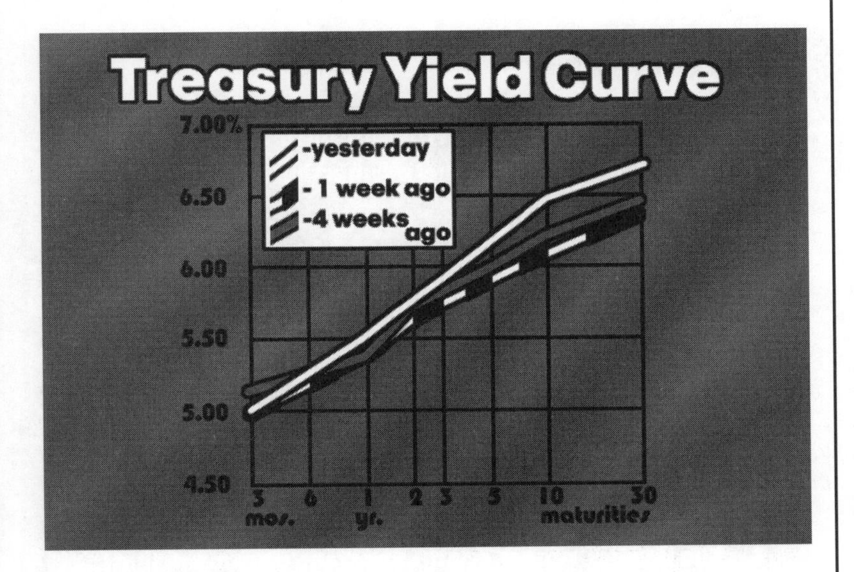

Yield curves graphically depict the relationship between interest rates and their maturities. The yield curve normally slopes upward, because long-term rates are generally higher than short-term. Therefore, when the yield curve is upward sloping, we refer to it as a "normal yield curve."

SUMMARY

- £ There are three main types of businesses: the sole proprietorship, the partnership, and the corporation.
- £ Taxes, liability, and the ability to raise capital are the main concerns in choosing a business formation.
- £ The overall goal of the financial manager and the company is to maximize shareholder wealth.
- £ The annual report is an important document that investors use to evaluate companies. Two of the most important statements in the annual report are the balance sheet and the income statement.
- £ The components of interest rates include the real rate, the inflation premium, and the risk premium.
- £ The term structure of interest rates is the relationship between long-term rates and short-term rates.

Quiz 1

1. The goal of the financial manager is to

   ____.

2. The three main types of businesses are

   ____________________, ____________________, and

   ____________________.

3. When deciding which business organization is best for them, potential business owners focus on

   ____________________ and ____________________.

4. The ease of formation and relief from taxes at the entity level are two advantages to ____________________ and

   ____________________.

5. ____________________ are held liable only for their amount of investment in the business, but have no power over the day-to-day operations.

6. The owners of a corporation are called

   ____________________.

STUDY SIDEKICK

7. The three main advantages of corporations are
_______________, _______________, and
_______________.

8. The earnings of a corporation divided by the number of outstanding shares is called the _______________.

9. The greater the expected cash flow of a business, the greater the _______________; and therefore, the greater the value of the stock.

10. Three of the factors that determine and affect the market price of a stock are _______________,
_______________, and _______________.

11. The money that a business holds onto for investment in new projects and machinery is known as
_______________.

12. Everyone has a boss. The CEO of a corporation reports to the _______________, who is responsible to the
_______________.

13. Conflicts that occur when managers put their own interest ahead of the corporation's interest are known as
_______________.

QUIZ

14. The ______________ is the basic accounting equation that sets assets equal to liabilities plus owners' equity.

15. The most important financial document that businesses produce is the ________________.

16. Stockholders who do not have voting rights but do have fixed dividend payments are known as ____________ stockholders.

17. The _________________________ reviews a business's earnings over a set period.

18. The symbol __________ represents the quoted market rate of interest.

19. The quoted rate of interest consists of the ___________________, the ______________, and the ______________________.

20. The ____________, symbolized by _________, is the rate on a riskless security and does not exist in the real world.

21. Symbolized by RP, the ____________________ is added to compensate for the perceived riskiness of an investment.

22. The ____________________ is calculated by combining the real rate of return and the inflation premium. It is represented by the symbol __________.

23. ____________________ are used to graphically depict the relationship between interest rates and their maturities. It is normally _____________ sloping.

24. The three types of U.S. Treasury securities are the ____________, ______________, and _________________.

25. When studying the term structure of interest rates you will note that historically, __________ rates are typically greater than _______________ rates.

If you answered most of the questions right, good job!!

If you got a few wrong, don't fret. Just buy a brand-new workbook and take the test again!!!

Time Value of Money

0:36:00

The value of money changes over time. For example, $100 is worth much more today than it will be worth ten years from now.

0:36:48

Section A: Future Value

Future value is the amount that a present sum of money will grow to in the future when compounded at a certain interest rate.

Here's an easy example of future value. You deposit $10,000 in your savings account—which surely happens all the time. The account has an interest rate of 8% a year.

$10,000 at 8% = $10,800

In a year, that $10,000 will be worth $10,800. The future value of that money when put in a savings account is $10,800, or $800 more than the present value.

Compounding interest happens when interest is added to a balance (or **principal**) at regular intervals over a certain period. *Compounding is charging interest on interest.* In other words, you start with a principal balance, and interest is added at the end of a certain period of time. At the end of the next period interest is added again, but this time the interest added is calculated from the total balance—the original principal plus the accumulated interest.

Let's look at it from a debt perspective, which you may be more familiar with. Let's say you spent $5,000 on your credit card at a local mall. You reach your $5,000 limit all in one day. Let's say this card compounds your interest at 15% interest once a year.

$$\begin{array}{r} 5000 \\ \times\ 0.15 \\ \hline 750 \end{array}$$

So if you spend 5 grand on goodies, at a yearly rate of 15%, then at the end of a year you would owe $5,750. You are paying $750 in interest for that year on a principal of $5,000.

Last week, I woke up at six a.m. because this couple was having a screaming fight on the street outside my house. So I opened the window, and sat down, and listened.
— Anne Scoville

Compounding: The Long Way

If you put $2,000 in the bank, with 10% interest compounded yearly, and you left the money in the bank for three years, how much would you have at the end of the third year? Remember, interest is compounded on interest after the first year. Let's figure it out.

$2,000 times 10% for the first year equals $200. $2,000 plus $200 equals $2,200. Then you compound $2,200 at 10% for the second year. $2,200 times 10% equals $220. $2,200 plus $220 equals $2,420. Then you compound $2,420 at 10% for the third and final year. $2,420 times 10% equals $242. $2,420 plus $242 for the third and final year equals $2,662. The future value of $2,000 in the bank for three years compounded yearly equals $2662. So you would make $662.

The Calculations

2,000

2,000(10%) = 200

2,000 + 200 = 2,220

2,200(10%) = 220

2,200 + 220 = 2,420

2,420(10%) = 242

2,420 = 2,662

Pretty exhausting, huh? Don't you think there's an easy way? Read on, friends.

Compounding: The Not-So-Long Way

There's a way to shorten this process. We can say future value (FV) is equal to present value (PV) times one, plus the interest rate (i) raised to the nth power (the number of periods).

$$FV = PV\,(1 + i)^n$$

This future value equation essentially adds the interest for each period to the existing balance, before compounding that interest again for the next period. The $(1 + i)^n$ portion of the equation is a shortcut so that you do not have to add each and every **compounding period**. However, there is an even shorter shortcut to calculating future value.

Compounding: The Short Way

The $(1 + i)^n$ portion of the future value equation is called the **future value interest factor (FVIF)**. To determine the FVIF for a particular scenario, refer to Table Uno. (See the Other Important Stuff section in the back of the workbook!) Find the interest rate along the horizontal row on top, and the number of periods along the left vertical column. The FVIF is where those two points intersect. Simply multiply the FVIF number by the present value to determine the future value.

So the future value equation can be rewritten as:

FV = PV [FVIF(interest rate, periods)].

CAUTION

A word of caution: *Interest is not always compounded annually.* Therefore, when using compounding interest you must be aware of how often the compounding occurs. The future value equation above is based on annual interest compounding. However, many institutions choose to compound interest more frequently. The compounding period can have a severe effect on the future value of an investment.

For example, when compounding interest semiannually, the given interest rate must be divided by two to obtain the interest per compounding period. The number of years must also be multiplied by two to determine the correct number of compounding periods (because there are two periods per year when compounding semiannually).

If you had an investment with a present value of $100 and it was compounded semiannually for a total of 10 years at a 10% annual rate, you would actually have twenty periods of compounding at 5% per period. When you fill in your formula, you must count the number of periods, not the number of years, and apply the appropriate interest per period.

So the future value of this investment is equal to the $100 present value, multiplied by the FVIF. The FVIF is measured by interest and periods.

$$\textbf{FV} = \textbf{100 [FVIF(interest, periods)]}$$

In 10 years, your investment will be compounded semiannually for 20 periods. If the annual rate is 10% per year, you have a 5% rate per period, because there's two periods in every year. All you need to do is look at Table Uno and find where the 20th period and 5% interest meet. They meet at 2.653. Multiply 2.653 times the present value.

$$\textbf{PV} = \textbf{100 (2.653)}$$

You get 265.30. Super duper! Woo.

0:48:05

Section B: Future Value of an Annuity

An **annuity** is a stream of equal payments made over a certain period of time at fixed intervals. There are two main types of annuities: the **ordinary annuity** and the **annuity due**.

The difference between an ordinary annuity and an annuity due is when the payment occurs. An ordinary annuity is one in which the payment occurs at the end of the period. Ordinary annuities are the most common.

An annuity due is an annuity whose payment is made at the beginning of the period. Unlike the ordinary annuity, the annuity due is quite rare in the financial world.

Annuities with the FVIFA

To calculate the future value of an ordinary annuity, use the following equation:

FVannuity = PAY [FVIFA(interest, periods)]

FVIFA represents the future value interest factor of an annuity. The value of FVIFA can be found in Table Dos. (Once again, Table Dos can be found in the Other Important Stuff section.) Table Dos is similar to Table Uno. To determine the value of FVIFA, look at Table Dos for the interest rate along the top horizontal row, and then look for the number of compounding periods listed vertically. Where these two points intersect is the FVIFA. Then you simply follow the formula just stated and multiply the FVIFA value by the payment, or PAY. The result is the future value of the annuity.

If you had an annuity with $600 yearly payments, and the current interest rate was 6%, what would be the value of the annuity in five years?

In this example, we go to Table Dos, look for the interest rate of 6%, and then look for the number of periods, 5 (once again stated annually, so a period equals one year). Five periods and 6% intersect at 5.637. This is the FVIFA—the future value interest factor of an annuity. Then we take the FVIFA and multiply it by the payment of $600.

$$\begin{aligned} \textbf{FVannuity} &= \textbf{PAY[FVIF(interest, periods)]} \\ &= \textbf{600[FVIF(6\%,5)]} \\ &= \textbf{600(5.637)} \\ &= \textbf{3,382.20} \end{aligned}$$

The future value of this annuity is $3,382.20.

The process for calculating the future value of an annuity due is slightly different because the annuity due's payment occurs at the beginning of the period rather than at the end. Therefore, we must add one more compounding payment, or multiply the FVIFA by one, plus the interest rate. This will increase the compounding periods by one without increasing the number of payment periods.

Annuity Due

To calculate the future value of an annuity due, use the following modified equation:

FVannuity due = PAY (FVIFA) (1 + i)

Using the same numbers from the example above, we would have 600 times 5.637, which is the FVIFA, times 1.06, which is 1 plus i.

FVannuity due = 600 (5.637) (1.06) = 3,585.13

This deposit will now equal $3,585.13 in its new life as an annuity due.

SUMMARY

- **Annuity due payments are made at the beginning of the period, so they get compounded one more time.**
- **Regular (deferred) annuities pay out at the end of the period.**

Fun Fact: *If you holler the word "annuity" as loud as you can in a public place, people will often turn and say, "Gesundheit." If you holler it again, they will escort you out of the building.*

0:54:40

Section C: Present Value

Present value is the next tool you will need to decipher the mysteries of finance.

Any amount of money in the future can buy fewer things than the same amount can now. Present value allows you to adjust for the devaluation of money over time. Present value gives you the value of a future sum in present-day dollars.

If you know how many dollars you'll have in the future, present value can tell you how much they would buy today.

Future and present value are very different concepts. Unfortunately, they're related mathematically. Present value is the inverse of future value. Future value compounds by an interest rate; present value discounts by an interest rate. Present value essentially takes away the interest.

To calculate the value of some future sum in present-day dollars, we turn the future value equation upside down.

The equation used to calculate present value is:

$$\mathbf{PV} = \frac{\mathbf{FV}}{(\mathbf{1} + i)^n}$$

PVIF

Present value discounts the funds to be received in the future to determine what they are worth in present-day dollars. The one over $(1 + i)^n$ portion of the present value equation is known as the present value interest factor, or PVIF. Using Table Tres, you

can easily determine the PVIF value. Again, Table Tres lists the interest rates along the top row and the number of periods along the bottom. (You can find it in the Other Important Stuff section.) By finding the point at which the two intersect, you can determine the PVIF value. Because of this shortcut, we can rewrite the present value equation as the following:

PV = FV [PVIF(interest, periods)]

Because present value takes away the interest, it's also useful when you know how many dollars you want in the future, and you know what the interest rate is, but you don't know how many dollars to invest.

Financial managers and investors use the present value equation frequently to determine the true value of potential investments.

Here's an example for you. Let's say you want to have $100,000 in ten years to purchase a ship. You found a good investment will give you a return of 10%. How much do you need to invest today to make $100,000 in ten years? What you're really going to find is the present value of the $100,000 in ten years, discounted at 10%. Let's stick the numbers into the formula.

PV = FV [PVIF(interest, periods)]
PV = 100,000 [PVIF(10%, 10)]
PV = 100,000 (0.3855)
PV = 38,550

With the numbers plugged into our formula, present value equals 100,000 times the PVIF of 10% interest and 10 periods,

or 100,000 times 0.3855. We know this by looking at our handy Table Tres for tenth period and 10% interest. 100,000 times 0.3855 equals 38,550.

To whoever finds this note: I have been imprisoned by my father who wishes me to marry against my will. Please please please please come and rescue me. I am in the Tall Tower of swamp castle. — John Cleese, *Monty Python and The Holy Grail*

You would have to invest $38,550 in that security for ten years at a 10% interest rate to make $100,000. $38,550 is the present value, or the value today.

Opportunity cost is another concept that investors use, along with present value, when analyzing investments.

Opportunity Cost Rate

The **opportunity cost rate** is the rate of return for an alternative investment of similar risk. The rate of return that could have been earned on another, alternative investment is called the opportunity cost rate. If you were to find another investment of similar risk, its rate of return would be the opportunity cost rate (Do you get this yet? The opportunity cost rate is the rate of return you could have gotten on another investment of similar risk).

Financial managers and investors use the opportunity cost rate as a method of comparing expected returns or **discount rates** of potential projects.

Section D: Present Value of an Annuity

0:58:25

As stated earlier, an annuity is a steady stream of payments over a given period. Because of the time value of money, each subsequent payment of an annuity is worth less. By calculating the present value of an annuity, we can determine how much all of the payments are worth in today's dollars.

PVIFA

To calculate the **present value** of an ordinary annuity, use the present value formula and Table Quatro (see the Other Important Stuff section). Table Quatro will provide you with a value for the present value interest factor of an annuity (or PVIFA) by finding where the interest rate and number of periods intersect. Once the value of PVIFA has been found, simply use the present value equation, adjusted for an annuity.

PV of Annuity = PAY [PVIFA(interest, periods)]

A good example of an annuity is the lottery. Let's say you won. You hit the big one, $10 million, which entitles you to $500,000 a year for 20 years. The current discount rate is 8%. Let's find the present value of this annuity.

PVannuity = Pay[PVIFA(interest, periods)]
= 500,000[PVIFA(8%,20)]
= 500,000(9.8181)
= 4,909,050

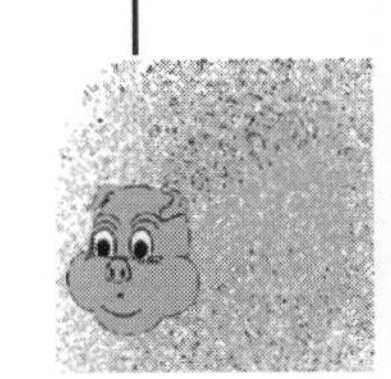

First, look at Table Quatro to get the PVIFA. Find 20, the number of periods (for 20 years). Then find 8%, the discount rate. They come together at a PVIFA of 9.8181. Then multiply 9.8181 times $500,000, or the annuity payment. You get 4,909,050. So the present value of that lottery win is $4.9 million.

PV of an Annuity Due

To compute the **present value** of an annuity due, you must make a similar adjustment as we did for the future value of an annuity due. You will recall that to calculate the future value of an annuity due, we added an additional discount period to the mix because the annuity payment is made at the beginning of each period. When calculating the present value of an annuity due, because we are discounting, we multiply the ordinary annuity from the tables by 1 plus the interest rate.

$$\textbf{PV of annuity due} = \textbf{PAY (PVIFA)} (1 + i)$$

Again, we use Table Quatro to determine the value of PVIFA by locating the interest rate and number of periods and then multiplying that value by the payment and again by 1 plus the interest rate.

$$\begin{aligned} \textbf{PVAD} &= \textbf{PAY[PVIFA(interest, periods)]} (1 + i) \\ &= 500{,}000\ (9.8181)\ (1 + 0.08) \\ &= 5{,}301{,}774 \end{aligned}$$

So for our example, we have the annual payment, which is now made on January 1. The 500,000 is multiplied by the PVIFA of 8% and 20 periods. The PVIFA is the same as in the previous example, 9.8181. Then we multiply that by 1 plus the interest rate, or 1 plus 0.08. Simplify that a little. Now we have 500,000 times 9.8181 times 1.08. The answer now is 5,301,774.

1:02:34

Section E: Perpetuities

An annuity with a constant, never-ending stream of fixed payments is called a **perpetuity**. An easy way to remember the definition of a perpetuity is to think of the word perpetual.

To calculate the present value of a perpetuity, divide the payment by the interest rate or discount rate.

One afternoon, your kindhearted Uncle Stoli has a triple aneurysm in his home. Uncle Stoli's will is read and you are the sole heir to the Horseapple dynasty. Included in the will is a payment to you of 250,000 U.S. dollars every year until you die.

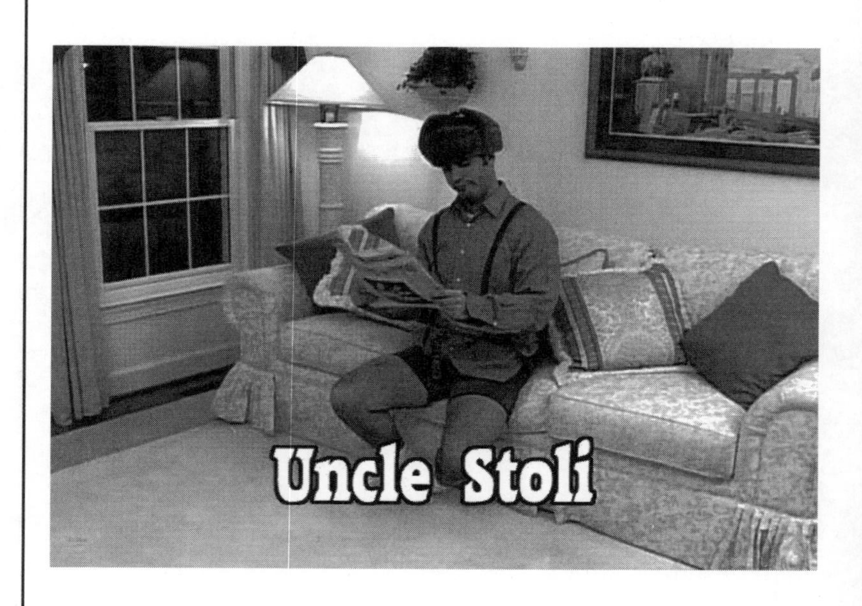

Let's figure out the value of this perpetuity. The payment is 250,000 dollars a year, and the current interest rate is 10%.

$$\textbf{PV perpetuity} = \frac{\textbf{PAY}}{i}$$

To set that up, we see the present value of the perpetuity is equal to the payment, 250,000, divided by the interest rate, 10%. That equals 2.5 million dollars, the present value of the perpetuity.

$$\frac{250{,}000}{0.10} = 2{,}500{,}000$$

A perpetuity is a fixed payment; therefore, the present value of the perpetuity depends on the going discount rate because the payment remains the same regardless of variations in market interest rates. If the discount rate *increases,* the present value of a perpetuity *decreases,* and vice versa.

> Note: If all of Paul McCartney's songs adhered to this rule, "the love you take would be *inversely proportional* to the love you make," which really makes for a horrible lyric.

So throughout all this, we've been saying that money is worth less in the future, and we showed you how to use all kinds of tools that work on that principle. But we're sure you're still wondering: WHY?

The whole idea is that everybody else out there, from investors to your mom, isn't just going to keep his or her money in a jar underneath a mattress. They're going to invest it, at market rates, which means they're all going to get a certain rate of return. They're all going to have more dollars in the future. This starts a chain reaction which eventually leads to higher prices, and thus money buys less.

KEEP IN MIND that this is a very simplistic way of explaining things—there's a billion other things that contribute to the **valuation** of money. But we at least wanted to start you off on the right track.

Section F: Different Interest Rates

1:05:53

%
Interest

Several different types of interest rates exist in the marketplace. It's important to understand the definitions of some of the more common interest rates and the differences between them.

The Nominal Rate

The market or nominal rate is the rate inherent in the market. This is the interest rate that lenders or borrowers quote you. It is usually stated as an annual rate. However, the nominal rate provides only a glimpse of what the actual interest will add up to. Compounding is the key to determining what will actually be owed or received. Therefore, the nominal rate is often accompanied by the number of compounding periods per year.

The APR

The **annual percentage rate (APR)** is another interest rate term. This term most frequently associated with credit cards. APR is essentially just another way of saying the nominal annual interest rate.

The **periodic rate** is the interest rate that is actually paid per compounding period. It is the nominal rate divided by the number of compounding periods per year. Lenders use the periodic rate whenever a payment is required every month, such as for car loans. Credit card companies also use the periodic rate on their statements to illustrate the interest charged to the borrower per period.

The EAR

The true rate that a borrower will end up paying on a loan or credit card is the **effective annual rate (EAR)**. EAR is the interest that will be paid for one year, including all compounding. To calculate your total interest rate for a year, use the following equation:

$$\mathbf{EAR} = \left(1 + \frac{i}{m}\right)^m - 1$$

The EAR accounts for all of the compounding interest for one year. Therefore, using the EAR equation will ensure that you calculate your total interest.

A credit card charging 2% interest a month, or a nominal rate of 24% a year, would work out like this:

EAR equals 1 plus the nominal rate of 24% divided by the number of compounding periods per year (12, because it's monthly) raised to the 12th power (for the number of compounding periods) minus 1.0.

$$\begin{aligned} \mathbf{EAR} &= \left(1 + \frac{i}{m}\right)^m - 1 \\ &= \left(1 + \frac{0.24}{12}\right)^{12} - 1 \\ &= (1.02)^{12} - 1 \\ &= (1.26824) - 1 \\ &= 0.2684 \end{aligned}$$

This equals 0.26824, or almost 27% a year. The credit card company may tell you 2% a month, but that compounding interest nails you with a 27% interest rate each year. You must use the EAR to truly determine an annual rate.

1:09:26

Section G: Compounding: The Master Formula

One single equation can be used to determine the future value of an investment no matter how many compounding periods there are. This equation can be used to calculate the future value of any investment whether interest is compounded daily, semiannually, or annually. This master equation is

$$\mathbf{FV} = \mathbf{PV}\ (\mathbf{1} + \frac{i}{m})^{mn}$$

All that you need to use this master formula is the present value (PV), the number of compounding periods per year (m), the number of years held (n), and the nominal interest rate (i). Simply plug these values into the equation, and do the math to determine the future value of any investment.

An example would be a quarterly compounded security which costs you $500 with a nominal interest rate of 10%. You will hold this investment for 10 years. Plug in the numbers.

$$\mathbf{FV} = \mathbf{PV}\left(\mathbf{1} + \frac{i}{m}\right)^{mn}$$

$$\mathbf{FV} = \mathbf{500}\left(\mathbf{1} + \frac{\mathbf{0.10}}{\mathbf{4}}\right)^{\mathbf{4(10)}}$$

$$= \mathbf{500\ (1.025)^{40}}$$

$$= \mathbf{500(2.68506)}$$

$$= \mathbf{1{,}342.53}$$

The future value is equal to \$500, the initial investment, times 1 plus 0.10 (the interest rate) over 4 (the number of periods per year), that quantity to the power of 4 times 10, which is the period per year times the number of years. So that's 500 times 1.025 to the power of 40.

The future value of this investment is equal to \$1,342.53.

Woo!!

1:12:00

Section H: Other Important Concepts

- $ Most bus lines run in both directions.
- $ Cutting boards are the germiest parts of the kitchen.
- $ Smaller jalapeños are spicier than bigger ones.

Irregular Cash Flows

Cash flows are not always regular. In many businesses (like retail), cash flows are irregular. To calculate the future value of an uneven cash flow, a version of the future value formula is used. Each and every cash payment is calculated separately with its own period. Then, all of those are totaled. We are essentially calculating future value the long way. Since we can't use the FVIF once for all of the cash flows like we did with regular payments, we must apply the FVIF to each payment according to the payment's period and the interest rate.

Over the next four years, we're getting payments of $200, $300, $500, and $600. The interest rate is 8%. So, for each part of the equation, we find the FVIF by cross-referencing the interest rate, 8%, and the number of periods, which changes depending on how long the money has been in the bank.

$$FV = 200(FVIF[8\%, 3]) + 300(FVIF[8\%,2]) + 500(FVIF[8\%,1]) + 600$$

$$= 200(1.260) + 300(1.166) + 500(1.080) + 600$$

$$= 1{,}741$$

So the $200 is compounded at 8% for three periods, the $300 is compounded at 8% for two periods, and the $500 is compounded at 8% for one period, and the $600 isn't compounded. Why not? These are cash flow payments, which happen at the end of the year. The last payment doesn't have a chance to get compounded before getting to you. Once you get all these figures, add them all together. Your final answer is $1,741.80.

Quiz 2

1. ____________________ is the amount that a present sum of money will grow to in the future when compounded by an interest rate.

2. ________________ occurs when interest is added to a balance at regular intervals over a period of time.

3. FV is equal to ________________________.

4. The future value interest factor, abbreviated as ________, is the ___________ portion of the future value formula.

5. When you compound interest semiannually, the interest rate must be __________________ and the number of periods must be ________________.

6. A stream of equal payments made over a period of time at fixed intervals is a(n) _____________.

7. An _____________________ is an annuity whose payments are made at the beginning of the period.

QUIZ

8. The formula used to calculate the future value of an ordinary annuity is ____________________.

9. The formula used to calculate the future value of an annuity due is ________________________.

10. Financial managers use the ______________________ concept to determine what an investment's value is today based on its future income projections.

11. $\frac{FV}{(1 + i)^n}$ is the ___________________ equation.

12. PVIF is the ____________ portion of the PV equation.

13. The _________________________________ is the rate of return for an alternative investment of similar risk.

14. The formula used to calculate the present value of an annuity is _____________________.

15. The modified formula used to calculate the present value of an annuity due is ________________________.

STUDY SIDEKICK

16. An annuity with a constant, never-ending stream of fixed payments is called a ________________.

17. The formula used to calculate the ____________________________ is $PV = \frac{PAY}{i}$.

18. The __________________ interest rate is inherent in the marketplace and is often quoted by lenders or borrowers.

19. The ___________________, abbreviated as _______, is the true rate that you'll end up paying on a loan or credit card. It is the interest paid over a year including all compounding.

20. The interest that is actually paid per compounding period is called the _______________________.

21. $\left(1 + \frac{i}{n}\right)^n - 1$ is the equation used to calculate the _______________________ and is abbreviated as ________.

22. The master equation that can be used to calculate the future value of any investment regardless of how interest is compounded is ___________________________.

QUIZ

23. In many businesses such as retail, ________________ are not always regular.

24. To calculate the future value of an uneven ____________________, a version of the ____________________ formula is used.

25. When calculating uneven cash flows, there is no shortcut. Each and every cash payment is calculated separately, with its own ______________________, and then they are all ______________________.

Correct answer = 1 point. Incorrect answer = 1 point. Add these two figures and purchase that many workbooks. Then eat some pop rocks.

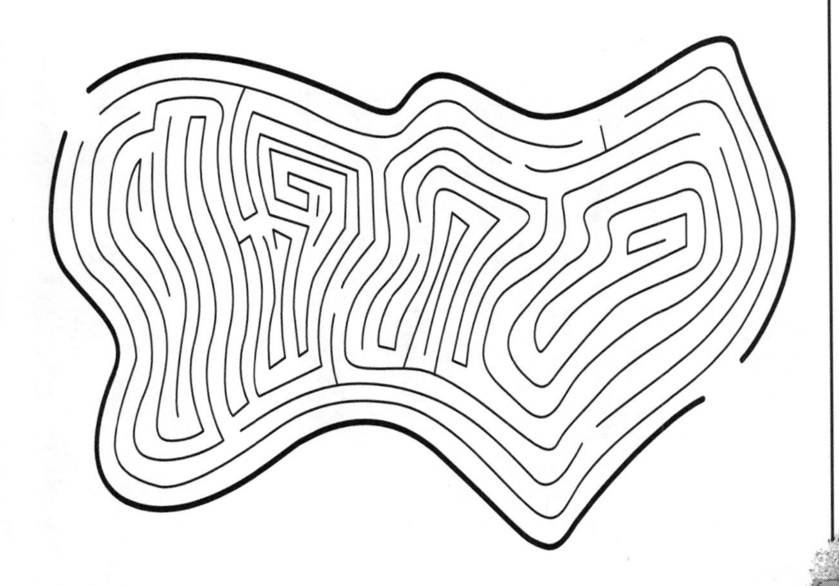

1:14:21

Basic Financial Concepts

1:14:30

Section A: Risk

Risk is the difference between expected and actual returns. It is the chance that what you expect to occur won't. Investors are always trying to minimize their risk while maximizing the rate of return on their investments.

Every action poses some type of risk. Every investment includes some type of risk. Investors try their best to minimize risk.

Risk aversion is the term used to describe a dislike for risk. Some people are less willing to take a risk than others, which means that they are more risk averse than their peers. People who are risk averse require a greater rate of return on any investments that they consider risky.

Investors who are indifferent to risk are called **risk neutral**. Risk neutral individuals are more likely to take risks with a low rate of return, because risk doesn't bother or excite them.

Investors who seek out risk are called **risk takers**.

STUDY SIDEKICK

Virtually all investments include some form of risk. The only securities considered risk-free are government securities. Government securities like T-bonds are considered risk-free because the U.S. government guarantees the rate of return on the investment.

Stock, however, does not have a guaranteed rate of return. Because so many different factors affect the value of stocks, you have no way of knowing what you will earn on your investment from day to day. You can, however, determine the **expected rate of return** for a stock, to better judge its worth. To determine the expected rate of return on a security you must assess the likelihood of obtaining a range of returns.

This is f'in' good ham. — Bruce McCullogh, *The Kids in the Hall*

Section B: Probability and Rate of Return

1:16:10

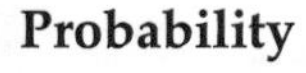

Probability

Probability is essentially another way of saying chance.

A **probability distribution** is a listing of all possible outcomes and the probability of each one. To calculate the expected rate of return on a particular stock, you must look at all possible outcomes for the investment based on the probability of those outcomes occurring.

Rate of Return

The **expected rate of return** is a weighted average of all possible returns or outcomes of an investment; the weight is the probability that each return will occur. The following formula calculates the expected rate of return on an investment:

$$\mathbf{K\^{} = P_1\,(O_1) + P_2\,(O_2) + P_3\,(O_3)}$$

This formula multiplies each outcome by the probability of that outcome occurring. K^, the symbol used to represent the expected rate of return, is equal to the sum of the probability of each outcome, multiplied by the outcome itself.

For instance, we choose to invest in a company called Nuggets, Inc. Nuggets produces the colored deodorizer disks placed at the bottom of urinals. This product is referred to as "nuggets."

There are three possibilities for the economy: A boom , which is high economic activity; a normal period; or a recession, which is low economic activity. Each, as you can see from

the chart, has its own probability of occurring. We made the probabilities up for this example. Your professors will make up different ones for you.

Period	Probability	Return
Boom	20%	20%
Normal	60%	10%
Recession	20%	0%

Taking our Nuggets example, in a boom economy, which has a 20% chance of occurring, the return on Nuggets' stock is pouring in at 20%. In a normal period, at a 60% chance of occurring, the return is trickling in at 10%; and in a recession, at a 20% chance of occurring, the return is poor, at 0%.

$$\begin{aligned} K_s &= 0.20(0.20) + 0.60(0.10) + 0.20(0) \\ &= 0.04 + 0.06 + (0) \\ &= 0.20 \end{aligned}$$

So take each probability, multiply it by its probable outcome, and then add it all up. You get an expected rate of return for Nuggets of 0.10, or 10 %.

Probability distributions can be plotted on a graph to visually demonstrate the variability of an investment's expected returns, based on differing states of the economy.

First, plot the probability of a particular state of the economy on the *y* (vertical) axis, and the rate of return for that same outcome on the *x* (horizontal) axis. Continue plotting points until you have represented all three possible states of the economy--a

boom, a normal period, and a recession. Once all of your returns for a particular investment have been plotted, you can connect the dots, drawing the curve of the continuous probability distribution. This distribution should resemble a bell curve.

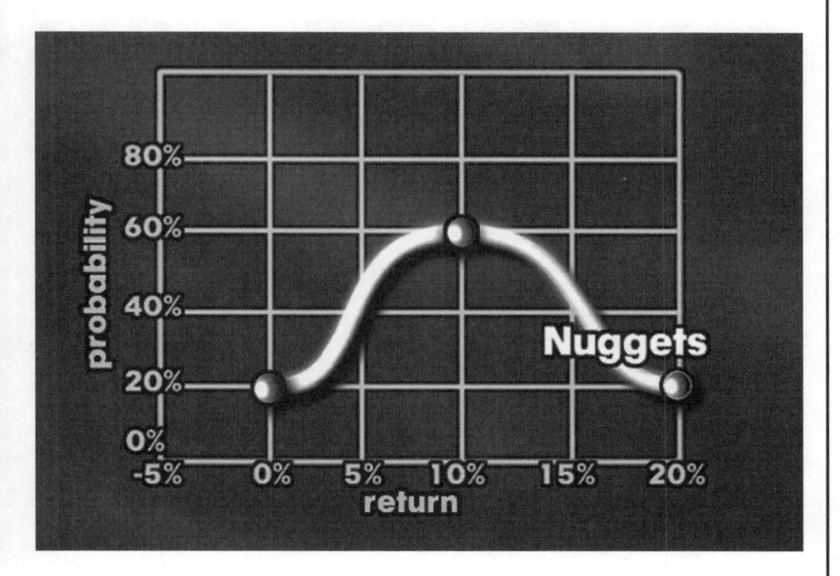

Probability distributions play an important role in investment analysis because even if two companies have the same expected rate of return, one could be a better investment than the other. One of the company's rates of return may be more susceptible to changes in the economy than another.

STUDY SIDEKICK

The narrower a stock's probability distribution is, the lower its risk. This is because a stock with a pointed distribution, such as that of Nuggets, would be less likely to have an actual return other than its expected return.

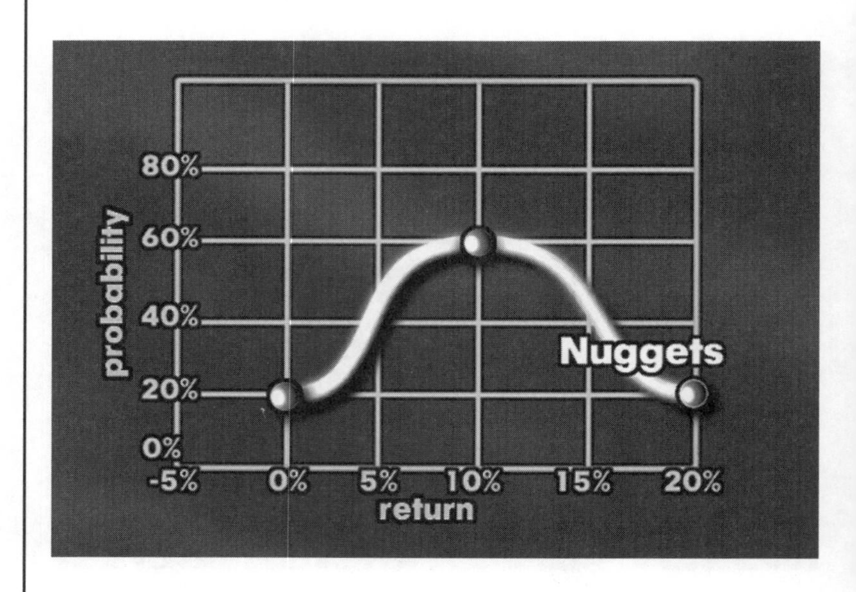

Video Notes

The probability distribution for Naked Trampolining is flatter and longer than that of Nuggets. Its returns fluctuate greatly depending on the state of the economy. Naked Trampolining's probability distribution is less pointy; therefore, more risk is involved in Naked Trampolining's stock.

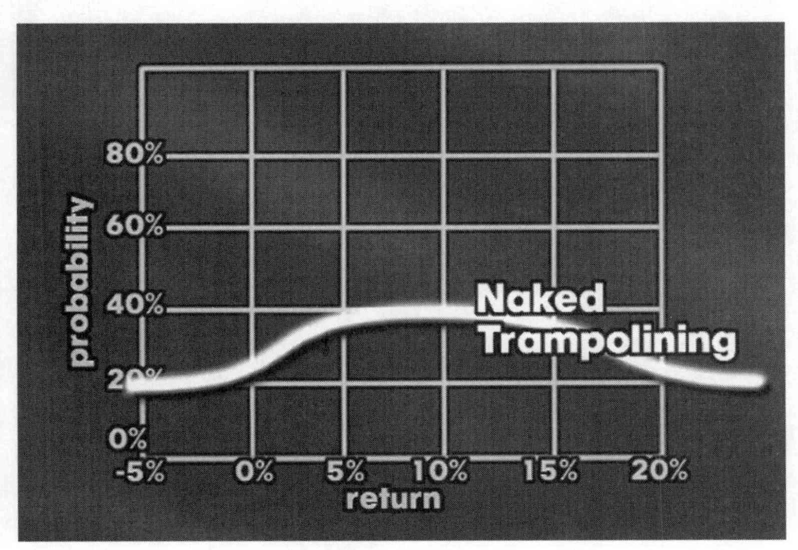

STUDY SIDEKICK

The probability distribution for H_2OCo (a water utility) is highly pointed because it is a utility. People require its service regardless of the state of the economy, so H_2OCo's rate of return hardly fluctuates at all.

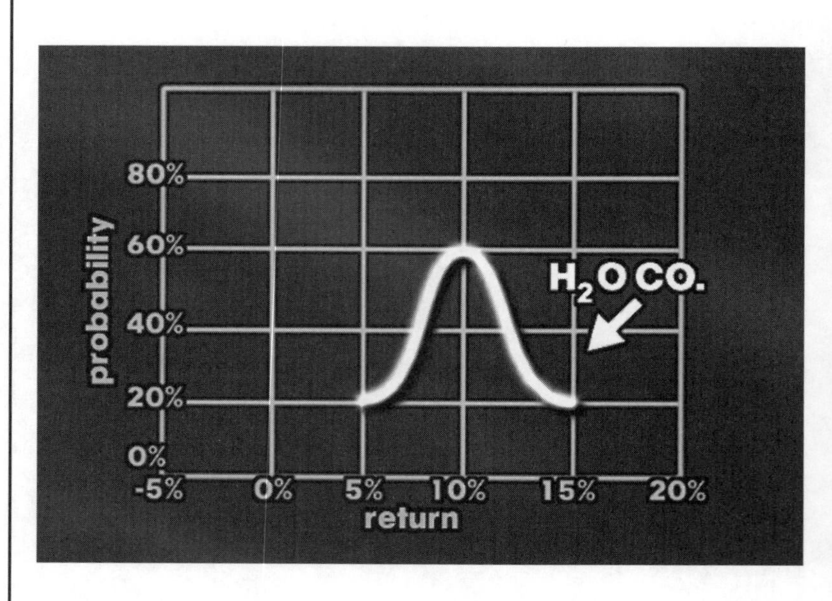

STANDARD DEVIANT FINANCIAL INFO:

The greater the chance of the expected rate of return being something other than the investor's required rate of return, the less pointed the probability distribution and the more risky the stock.

Section C: Risk and Standard Deviation

1:23:05

THE STANDARD DEVIANTS

Standard Deviation

Standard deviation is the statistical measurement of risk. It measures the difference between the expected return and actual return.

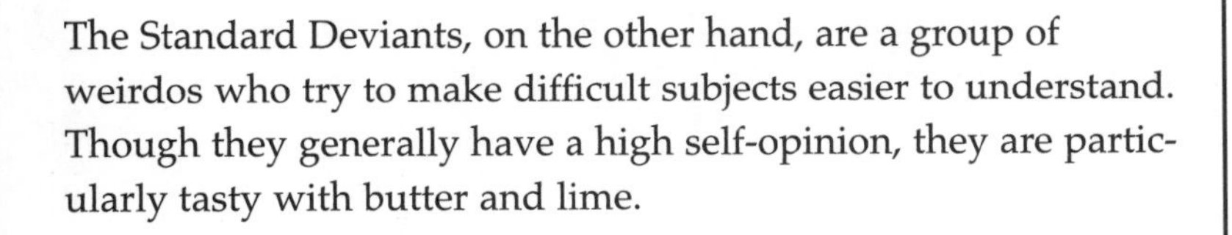

The Standard Deviants, on the other hand, are a group of weirdos who try to make difficult subjects easier to understand. Though they generally have a high self-opinion, they are particularly tasty with butter and lime.

As explained above, the more narrow and pointed the probability distribution, the less risky the investment. The standard deviation is a statistical measurement of the narrowness of the probability distribution, or the variability of possible returns. The smaller the standard deviation, the narrower the probability distribution, and the lower the risk.

Of our earlier examples, Naked Trampolining would have the highest standard deviation because it has the greatest variability and therefore the widest probability distribution. H_2OCo would have the lowest standard deviation because it has the least variability and narrowest probability distribution.

Here is the formula used to calculate the standard deviation of expected returns of a stock is.

$$\sigma = \sqrt{\Sigma(K_i + K\wedge)^2 P_i}$$

Study Sidekick

Standard deviation, or sigma, equals the square root of the sum of all of the differences between expected and actual outcomes squared $(Ki + K\^)^2$, each multiplied by their respective probability (P_i).

Let's try one. Just plug in the numbers from our Nuggets example as we go along. First we'll figure out the differences, then multiply them by their probabilities. Once we get those three, we'll sum them, and go on from there. Remember now, Nuggets' expected rate of return was 10%.

Boom: $\mathbf{20 - 10 = 10}$

$\mathbf{10^2 = 100}$

So, in a boom economy, Nuggets, Inc. has an actual return of 20%. 20% minus the expected return of 10% is 10. Square that, and we get 100.

Normal: $\mathbf{10 - 10 = 0}$

$\mathbf{0^2 = 0}$

In a normal period, Nuggets, Inc. showed a 10% return. 10 minus the expected return of 10 equals 0. 0 squared is 0.

Recession: $\mathbf{0 - 10 = -10}$

$\mathbf{-10^2 = 100}$

In a recession, the company showed a return of 0 percent. Zero minus 10 is negative 10. Negative 10 squared is 100.

So now you have three totals, one for each possible outcome. Following the formula, you take each of these and multiply it by the probability that state will occur.

Boom	**100(0.20)**	**= 20**
Normal	**0(0.60)**	**= 0**
Recession	**100(0.20)**	**= 20**

In a boom, 100 times 20% chance of occurring equals 20. In a normal economy, 0 times 60% chance of occurring is 0; and in a recession, 100 times 20% chance of occurring equals 20.

$$20 + 0 + 20 = 40$$

Now you take those final numbers and add them. This is the sum of the differences squared, times their probability. It's also called the **variance**.

$$\sqrt{40} \cong 6.32$$

When we take the square root of this number, we'll get the standard deviation, or s.

Coefficient of Variation

The **coefficient of variation** standardizes risk. In other words, you use the coefficient of variation to determine how many units of risk you have per unit of return.

The coefficient of variation takes the standard deviation and divides it by the expected rate of return to measure risk per unit of return.

STUDY SIDEKICK

The coefficient of variation is like putting a magnifying glass on the standard deviation to focus more clearly on the differences between two investments. To calculate the coefficient of variation, we use the following formula:

$$CV = \frac{\sigma}{K^{\wedge}}$$

The coefficient of variation is a convenient way to compare investments. Investments can have similar returns and standard deviations, and therefore can have a similar degree of risk.

Examining the coefficient of variation more closely, one investment may prove to be less risky per unit of return than the other. The lower the coefficient of variation, the better. Unlike standard deviation, the coefficient of variation is a whole number, not a percentage. The higher the number, the riskier the project.

The coefficient of variation is also referred to as the risk return trade-off because it measures risk per unit of return of your investment.

SUMMARY

£ **There are two measurements of risk for individual stock investments: standard deviation, which is the most basic statistical measurement of risk; and the coefficient of variation, which measures risk per unit of return. They are both important in finance.**

Quiz 3

1. Risk is the difference between ________________ and ____________________.

2. A dislike for risk is called ________________________.

3. Investors who are indifferent to risk are called ______________________.

4. Investors who seek risk are called ______________________.

5. The only securities considered risk-free are ______________________.

6. __________________ is another way of saying chance.

7. A ____________________________ is a list of all possible outcomes and the likelihood that each will occur.

QUIZ

8. The ____________________, abbreviated as ______, is a weighted average of all possible returns of an investment, with the weight being the probability that each return will occur..

9. $P_1(O_1) + P_2(O_2) + P_3(O_3)$ is the formula used to calculate the ____________________ of an investment.

10. The more pointed a stock's ________________, the lower its __________.

11. The statistical measurement of risk is ____________________, abbreviated as ________.

12. The smaller the ____________________, the ________________ the probability distribution and therefore, the ______________ the risk.

13. The formula used to calculate standard deviation is ____________________.

14. The number within the square root symbol in the standard deviation formula is known as the ________________.

Me, I like croutons. They make me tingly. I'm serious, David. I'm crou-tingly. — Tad Ghostal to David Byrne, Space Ghost Coast-to-Coast

STUDY SIDEKICK

15. The ______________________________ takes the standard deviation and divides it by the expected rate of return to measure risk per unit of return. It is an excellent means of comparing two investments.

16. The ___________ the coefficient of variation, the better the investment.

WHY BIG FAT PRETZELS ARE BETTER THAN SKINNY ONES

Big pretzels give you more pretzel for your money.

Big pretzels don't dry out and get stale.

Big pretzels aren't hawked by an annoying little pretzel man.

The salt doesn't fall off big pretzels.

You have to work really hard to finish a big pretzel. That way you feel the pretzel is worth the reward.

You can use those big fat pretzel rods to pretend you're smoking a cigar, and have little fear of getting lip cancer.

SUGGESTIONS FOR ALTERNATIVE USES FOR SMALL, SKINNY PRETZELS

Animal feed.

Mix with water: instant pretzel-mâché. Perfect for arts and crafts projects!

Kindling.

Grind into small pieces. Throw at weddings.

Glue together into planks. Construct model buildings and other structures.

Soak pretzels in perfume. Deposit them in closets and other musty areas to freshen the air.

VIDEO TIME CODE

The Wild and Wacky World of Finance Part 2

I. Dealing with more than one stock 0:03:16

A. Portfolios 0:03:40

1. Diversification 0:03:45
2. Expected rate of return on a portfolio 0:05:24
3. Portfolio effect 0:08:08
4. Correlation coefficient 0:08:30

B. CAPM 0:11:15

C. Beta 0:14:40

1. Market risk 0:15:15
2. Market beta = 1 .... 0:17:25
3. Beta of a portfolio 0:19:15

D. Putting CAPM to work for you 0:21:45

1. The formula 0:23:13
2. Using CAPM for required rate of return 0:25:45

E. Security market line 0:27:45

1. Constructing the SML 0:28:56
2. Using the SML 0:32:20

Study Sidekick

0:36:55 ...... **II. Stock and bond valuation**

0:38:28 ...... A. Terms

0:38:53 ...... 1. Par value

0:39:15 ...... 2. Coupon payment

0:39:25 ...... 3. Coupon rate

0:39:48 ...... 4. Market interest rate

0:40:08 ...... 5. Maturity date

0:40:18 ...... B. Bond present value

0:40:34 ...... 1. Determining current price

0:44:15 ...... 2. Shorter periods

0:46:00 ...... C. Discount and premium bonds

0:46:10 ...... 1. What's with interest rates

0:46:36 ...... 2. Discounts

0:49:23 ...... 3. Premiums

0:57:13 ...... 4. Current yield

0:53:18 ...... 5. Yield to maturity

0:55:25 ...... 6. Yield to call

0:59:20 ...... D. Stock valuation

1:00:00 ...... 1. Preferred stock

1:03:38 ...... 2. Constant growth stock: The Gordon Growth Model

1:09:20 ...... 3. Differential or supernormal growth stock

VIDEO NOTES

The Wild and Wacky World of Finance Part 2

Dealing with More Than One Stock

Section A: Portfolios

0:03:40

A **portfolio** is the assortment of securities held by an investor. Just as artists often have a big portfolio of art, rich guys often have a big portfolio of securities (as well as solid gold robots). Investors tend to hold more than one security to provide some **diversification**.

Diversification, or purchasing more than one security, lowers the total risk to an investor. When several investments are grouped together in a portfolio, it matters less what happens to each investment individually than what happens to the portfolio as a whole.

Because stocks do not always move in the same direction or react to the same circumstances, investors can reduce their investment risk by investing in a portfolio of securities as opposed to investing in simply one stock.

If an investor's portfolio consisted of only one stock, the investor would be concerned only with the return on that single security. In a portfolio of one stock, the standard deviation and coefficient of variation are appropriate measures of risk. However, since most investors diversify and add other assets or securities to their portfolios to reduce risk, the investor becomes concerned primarily with the return and risk of the portfolio as a whole. Every investment is analyzed for its effect on the risk and return of the portfolio.

Expected Rate of Return on a Portfolio

In addition to calculating the expected rate of return for a single stock, the well-diversified investor also needs to focus on the **expected return on a portfolio** of securities, which is represented by **K^p**. The expected return on a portfolio is equal to a weighted average of all the expected returns on each stock in

the portfolio. The weight is simply the portion of the total portfolio that each stock holds. The formula for calculating the expected return on a portfolio is

$$\mathbf{K^\wedge p = W_1K_1 + W_2K_2 + W_3K_3}$$

Let's say we've invested $1,000 in several companies. Of our total $1,000 investment, we have $400 in H_2OCo, which is 40% of our portfolio, and we have $300 in Nuggets, which equals 30%. Three hundred dollars in Porkers equals 30%. Together, all three stocks represent 100% of our portfolio. The expected rates of return for the companies are: H_2OCo 8%, Nuggets 10%, and Porkers 20%.

$$\mathbf{0.40(0.08) + 0.30(0.10) + 0.30(0.20) = 0.122}$$

The expected rate of return on the portfolio as a whole is 12.2 percent.

Portfolio risk is the risk involved in investing in a group of securities. A study of portfolio risk examines how various securities interact with one another. Investors seek a portfolio of investments that complement each other by maintaining a sort of inverse relationship. When one stock is performing poorly, another stock is performing well. Most investors include many different stocks in their portfolios to reduce the effect of a single poor investment. This effect is often achieved by investing in stocks from different industries.

Favorable interaction between stocks is known as the portfolio effect. If the stocks in a portfolio are moving in opposite directions, portfolio risk is being reduced.

Correlation Coefficient

The statistical measurement that illustrates how two components in a portfolio move together is called the **correlation coefficient,** or **r**. The correlation coefficient is a valuable tool for investors interested in maintaining a well-diversified portfolio.

The correlation coefficient can range from +1.0 to −1.0.

Positive 1.0 means that the two stocks in question are perfectly positively correlated, or that they always move together. On the other hand, a negative 1.0 means that the two stocks in question are perfectly negatively correlated, or that they always move in opposite directions. Obviously, for the investor who is attempting to diversify, two stocks with a correlation coefficient of +1.0 would not be good additions to the portfolio because they will respond in exactly the same way to certain economic factors. The less correlation, and the lower the correlation coefficient, the greater the benefits to the investor.

In reality, it is extremely rare for two stocks to have a correlation coefficient of −1.0 or +1.0. Nearly all stocks fall somewhere between the two and most have positive correlations, because most stocks respond favorably to a boom economy and poorly to a recession. The investor's goal is to reduce risk by selecting a portfolio of stocks with the lowest available correlations.

Section B: CAPM

Harry Markowitz and William Sharp designed a modeling procedure for analyzing the association between risk and rates of return for an investor. This formula is called the **capital asset pricing model (CAPM)**. CAPM is a specific formula that allows investors to determine the required rate of return on an investment, based on the risk that they will be taking. It is a general framework based on the concept that most investors are risk averse and expect to be rewarded for any risk that they take.

Markowitz

Sharp

As you increase the stocks in your portfolio, you can get rid of more and more of the risk inherent in the individual companies themselves, but you cannot eliminate all risk, because the companies move together based on the market. Even stocks in a portfolio as large as the New York Stock Exchange are affected by certain upturns and downturns in the economy. This type of risk, inherent in the market itself, is called **market** or **systematic risk**. Market risk affects everyone, and results from major world events like **inflation**, business cycles, monetary policy, or war.

If you have five stocks or fewer, you have a lot of risk. But if you buy a bunch of stocks (you diversify), you can get rid of some risk. This kind of risk is called **company-specific** or **unsystematic risk**. This risk is based on a company's own potential problems or situations like strikes, management, and poor financial strategies. Company-specific risks can be diversified away because they can be offset by events at another company in which you own stock.

STUDY SIDEKICK

Since the CAPM formula operates under the assumption that investors will diversify, it does not account for company-specific risk. Instead, the CAPM adjusts the rate of return based on how an investor's stock moves relative to the market. When you use CAPM to estimate the expected rate of return of investing in a stock, the amount of systematic risk a stock has relative to the entire market is what determines the risk of investing in that stock.

The **beta coefficient**, or β, measures how volatile a particular stock is relative to the volatility of the entire market portfolio.

Dewey Defeats Truman - A4 Weather - B1 Sports - C1 Income Summaries - D1

Todays Weather: [illegible]

The Standard Deviant

FINAL [illegible]

Thursday, September 31, 1998

WAR!!!

Market Rates Plummet

Risk Unchanged, Some Experts Blame War

New York (AP) Two [illegible] guys named Harry Markowitz and William Sharp designed a modeling procedure for analyzing the association between risk and rates of return for an investor.

This formula is called the Capital Asset Pricing Model - or CAP-M. CAPM is a specific formula that allows you to determine what risks you will take on investments while considering the investments' rates of return.

It is a general framework based on the concept that most investors are risk

Army Surprised

Dozens Startled, Many Soldiers Hide

NEW YORK—Legions of Belgian [illegible] stormed ashore Long Island today, beginning the invasion that has been feared for weeks.

"I wouldn't say we're scared." The President said in a news conference today.

"If we really thought the Belgians could kick our ass," he continued, "we'd be running to Omaha right now. As things are, the government of the United States of America feels perfectly comfortable [illegible]."

The Belgians found the shore relatively

Section C: Beta

0:14:40

The beta coefficient, represented by β, is the inclination of a stock to move with the market, or the tendency of a stock's return to move with the market's general return. When studying the concept of beta, remember that beta relates to how a stock moves relative to the movements of the market as a whole, and not to the actions of a specific organization.

The important thing is for you to *understand the concept* of beta. Although you *could* calculate beta, it will normally be supplied for you in your class. To calculate beta you would need a big-time huge computer with a bunch of programs and it's just a real pain. A bunch of brokerage companies publish betas, so why not get it from them? Know how to use beta, but don't sweat calculating it.

The beta of the market equals 1.0. If the individual stock being examined has a beta

equal to 1.0:	The stock has the same exact amount of risk as the market.
greater than 1.0:	The stock is considered riskier than the market.
less than 1.0:	The stock's risk is considered to be lower than that of the market.

Beta, not standard deviation, is a true measure of a stock's risk. Standard deviation provides an investor with the measurement of an individual stock's risk, but since many investors purchase a diverse portfolio, the risk of an individual stock is

not as important as how risky a given stock is relative to the portfolio. Beta is a measurement of a stock's relevant risk, because it provides the investor with a specific measure of risk compared to the market.

Beta of a Portfolio

Investors frequently use beta to determine how much the addition of a new stock will affect the risk of their portfolios. To calculate the beta of a portfolio, take the weighted average of the betas of the stocks in the portfolio.

The formula is

$$\beta_p = \mathbf{W_1\beta_1 + W_2\beta_2 + \ldots W_n\beta_n}$$

Here's an example:

H_2OCo totals $400, or 40% of the portfolio, Nuggets totals $300, or 30% of the portfolio, and Porkers totals $300, or 30% of the portfolio. H_2OCo has a beta of 0.6, Nuggets has a beta of 1.8, and Porkers has a beta of 2.2.

$$\begin{aligned}\boldsymbol{\beta_p} &= \mathbf{0.4(0.6) + 0.3(1.8) + 0.3(2.2)} \\ &= \mathbf{0.24 + 0.54 + 0.66} \\ &= \mathbf{1.44}\end{aligned}$$

The weight of H_2OCo (0.4) times H_2OCo's beta (0.6), plus Nuggets' weight (0.3), times Nuggets' beta (1.8), plus Porkers' weight (0.3), times Porkers' beta (2.2) equals 1.44.

Section D: Putting CAPM to Work for You

0:21:45

The capital asset pricing model, or CAPM, allows investors to determine what return they should receive on an investment, per level of beta or level of risk. This is also known as the **required rate of return**, because it is the rate that investors will require to invest in that particular stock.

To calculate the required rate of return on an investment using CAPM, several components are used: the beta of the stock, the risk-free rate in the market, and the expected return on the market. The CAPM formula is

$$\mathbf{K = K_{rf} + \beta\ (K_m - K_{rf})}$$

K, or the **required rate of return** for an individual security, is equal to the risk-free rate of return, plus the beta coefficient of the security, or β, times the expected market return minus the risk-free rate of return.

K_{rf}, or the **risk-free rate**, is the expected rate of return on long-term U.S. Treasury securities or bonds backed by the United States government.

K_m, or **market risk**, is the risk inherent in the market itself. Market risk affects all investors, and is the result of major world events such as inflation, business cycles, monetary policy, or war.

The CAPM formula allows investors to determine the risk-adjusted expected return on an individual stock. This rate is based on the risk premium of the market (K_m) minus the risk-free rate (K_{rf}).

Because market risk can not be diversified away (too bad, huh?), the required rate of return must be adjusted for it. The capital asset pricing model adjusts the rate of return based on how risky an individual stock is relative to the market.

The market's overall average risk minus the risk-free rate (the ($K_m - K_{rf}$) portion of the formula), is called the **market risk premium**. The market risk premium is the risk that the market, not an individual investment, requires above and beyond the securities that have no risk.

When multiplied by an individual stock's beta coefficient, the market risk premium gives investors their particular risk premium on that particular investment. The risk premium is the percentage above and beyond the risk-free rate that an investor will require to invest. The final step in the calculation of CAPM is to add that risk premium to the risk-free, or T-bill, rate to give you the required rate of return.

Therapets is a national chain of pet psychiatrists. The beta for Therapets is 2.6 (we got that number from an investment magazine, you guess which one). Because of this beta, we can tell that this company is much riskier than the market, but what return should we require if we make this investment? Use the CAPM formula.

$$K_s = K_{rf} + b\,(K_m - K_{rf})$$

$$K_s = 6 + 2.6(12-6)$$

$$K_s = 6 + 2.6(6)$$

$$K_s = 6 + 15.6$$

$$K_s = 21.6$$

STUDY SIDEKICK

The rate you require is equal to the risk-free rate plus the beta times the market risk premium. Fill in the blanks. K_s is equal to 6 plus 2.6 times 12 minus 6, which equals 6 plus 15.6, or 21.6. The required rate of return for Therapets is 21.6. So, because we're such frumpy, risk averse investors, we would require a very large rate of return on this risky investment.

Section E: Security Market Line

0:27:45

The **security market line (SML)** graphically depicts the capital asset pricing model. An example of a SML is shown here:

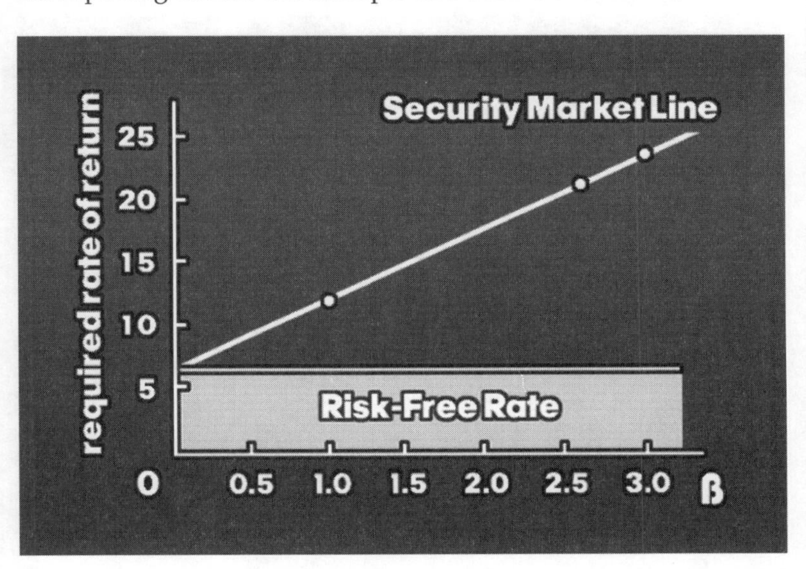

The required rate of return values are represented along the *y*-axis (vertical), and beta values are represented on the *x*-axis (horizontal).

The security market line is the diagonal line that graphs the relationship between risk and return for an individual security. Once enough securities have been plotted on the graph to draw the SML, an investor can use the graph to price securities by their beta alone.

The SML will be affected by changes in the rate of inflation and changes in risk aversion.

Increases in inflation will shift the SML upward.

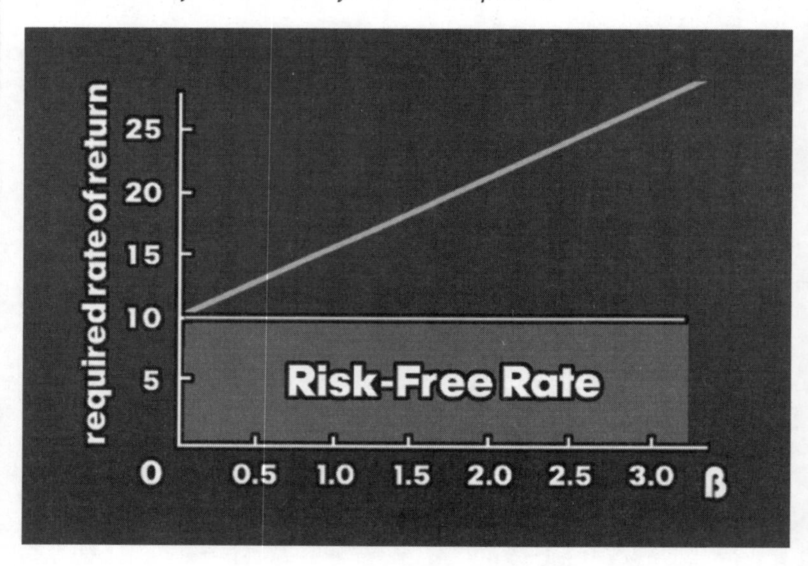

These changes will not change the slope of the line because inflation affects all parts of the SML equally. Inflation affects not only the rates of return on the investor's stocks, but on the market as a whole, including the risk-free rate. Therefore, as prices rise, the entire line shifts upward, parallel to the existing SML.

Changes in risk aversion will change the slope of the SML.

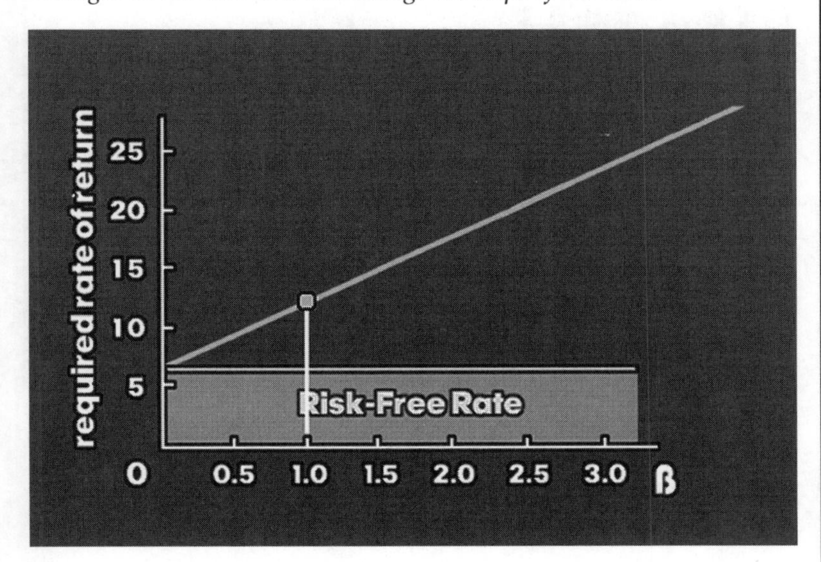

If investors in the market as a whole become more or less risk averse, they will require more or less return per unit of risk. This will cause the slope of the entire SML to change. As investors become more risk averse, their required rate of return per unit of risk increases. Therefore, the return on the market, or $\mathbf{K}_m$, increases while the risk-free rate, or $\mathbf{K}_{rf}$, remains the same.

Changes in the risk averseness do not affect the risk-free rate, because there is no risk premium in the risk-free rate. So, as investors become more risk averse, they require more return per unit of risk, increasing the slope of the security market line.

SUMMARY

The Security Market Line:

- **Can be used to price securities graphically.**
- **Is used to determine the expected return on an individual security based on a risk-free rate and a risk premium.**
- **Graphs CAPM.**

QUIZ

Quiz 4

1. ____________________, or purchasing more than one security, ____________ the overall risk to an investor.

2. Investors are concerned primarily with the ___________ and ___________ of their portfolios.

3. The ____________________________ is represented by K^p and is equal to the

____.

4. _______________________ is the risk involved in investing in a group of securities.

5. Favorable interaction between stocks is known as the

_________________________.

6. The statistical measurement that illustrates how two components in a portfolio move together is called the ________________________________, abbreviated as _______.

7. The goal for the investor is to reduce risk by selecting a portfolio of securities that have ___________ correlations.

8. ________________________________, abbreviated as _________, is a specific formula that allows investors to determine the required rate of return on an investment based on the risk that they will be taking.

9. $K = K_{rf} + (K_m - K_{rf})$ is the ______________ formula.

10. K_{rf}, or the ____________________, is the expected rate of return on a long-term U.S. Treasury security.

11. ________, or market risk, is the risk inherent in the market itself. It is the result of such things as _______________, ______________, and _______________.

12. _______________________ is the form of risk that can be diversified away.

13. The ________________________, abbreviated as _____, is the inclination of a stock to move in correlation with the market, or the tendency of a stock's return to move with the market's general return.

14. The **β** of the market is equal to __________.

Quiz

15. If a stock has a ___________ of greater than ______, it is considered ___________ than the market.

16. The market's overall average risk minus the risk-free rate ($K_m - K_{rf}$) is called the ______________________________.

17. The ______________________________, abbreviated as _______, is the diagonal line that graphs the relationship between risk and return for an individual security.

18. The SML is affected by changes in ___________________ and ___________________.

Whether you're right or wrong, confused or confident, it's never a bad idea to buy nineteen alternate workbooks.

PRACTICE EXAM I

At this point, we have gotten through half of the material we're going to teach you. So, what better place for a practice test? We've tried our best to simulate a midterm, so do *your* best to try not to cheat. The answers (with explanations) are at the back of the book.

1. Two major disadvantages of a corporation are:

a. they are difficult to form and changing ownership is difficult

b. they are difficult to form and they are double taxed

c. the owners have high liability and they are double taxed

d. it is difficult to form and dies when the board of directors dies

2. The president or CEO of a corporation reports to:

a. the treasurer

b. the CFO

c. the board of directors

d. the shareholders

TEST YOURSELF

3. The most important goal of the financial manager:

a. increase earnings

b. maintain small inventories with maximum profit

c. maximize shareholder wealth

d. increase profits

4. "Term structure of interest rates" refers to the relationship between:

a. long- and short-term interest rates

b. risky and riskless securities

c. the real rate of return and the inflation premium

d. high and low interest rates

5. History tells us that:

a. the greater the risk of a security, the lower the interest rate

b. the lower the risk of a security, the greater the interest rate

c. short-term interest rates are greater than long-term interest rates

d. long-term interest rates are greater than short-term interest rates

6. Which of the following could force a corporation into bankruptcy?

a. failure to pay common stockholders
b. failure to pay preferred stockholders
c. failure to pay bondholders
d. none of the above

7. Most stocks are traded on:

a. primary markets
b. secondary markets
c. credit markets
d. capital markets

8. Interest rates are made up of:

a. real rate and the inflation premium
b. the risk-free rate and the periodic rate
c. the risk premium
d. a and c
e. b and c
f. none of the above

TEST YOURSELF

9. To calculate the future value of a lump sum, multiply the present value times the:

a. FVIFA

b. FVIF

c. PVIF

d. PVIFA

10. To calculate the future value of an annuity due, multiply the present value times:

a. FVIF times $(1 + i)^{mn}$

b. FVIFA

c. FVIFA times $(1 + i)$

d. PVIF times $(1 + i)$

11. Which of the following statements is most true?

a. future value compounds by an interest rate and present value discounts by an interest rate

b. future value discounts by an interest rate and present value compounds by an interest rate

c. future value and present value compound by an interest rate

d. none of the above

12. What statements appear in most annual reports?

a. income statement

b. balance sheet

c. statement of cash flows

d. statement of retained earnings

e. all of the above

f. a and b

13. You won the lottery and were awarded $6.5 million to be paid over the next 20 years. You will receive $325,000 each year for 20 years. How much is that $6.5 million prize really worth today when today's interest rate is 7%?

a. $6,500,000

b. $6,045,000

c. $3,443,050

d. $2,282,670

14. You have decided to start saving for a new car. You know that you can get the car you want for $6,500. So, you discipline yourself to deposit $1,500 at the end of each year for 4 years in an account that earns 7% interest. Will you have enough money to buy your car at the end of the 4 years?

a. yes

b. no

c. not enough information to determine

TEST YOURSELF

15. What if you deposit the same $1,500 mentioned in question 14 at the beginning instead of the end of each year for 4 years? How much will you have at the end of the 4 years?

a. $11,322.30

b. $8,236.50

c. $6,660.00

d. $7,126.20

16. A correlation coefficient of +1.0 means:

a. two stocks are opposite the market beta

b. two stocks are perfectly positively correlated

c. two stocks are equal to the market beta

d. two stocks are perfectly negatively correlated

17. What is the present value of a 20-year, ordinary annuity of $500 with a 6% expected return?

a. $5,734.96

b. $4,650.17

c. $10,000.00

d. $6,079.04

e. none of the above

18. Using the same information as in question 17, but with semiannual compounding, what is the present value of the annuity?

a. $7,438.75

b. $7,523.15

c. $9,320.04

d. $11,557.39

e. none of the above

19. The interest rate that lenders and borrowers typically quote is the:

a. effective annual rate

b. nominal rate

c. periodic rate

d. none of the above

20. The master equation for compounding interest to determine future value is:

a. $PV\left(1 + \frac{i}{m}\right)^{mn}$

b. $\left(1 + \frac{i}{m}\right)^{m} - 1$

c. $PV\ (1 + i)^{n}$

d. PAY (FVIFA)

e. none of the above

TEST YOURSELF

21. Which statement is most true?

a. as the discount rate decreases, the present value of a perpetuity decreases

b. as the discount rate increases, the present value of a perpetuity increases

c. as the discount rate increases, the present value of a perpetuity decreases

d. none of the above

22. What is the present value of a perpetuity that promises to pay $150,000 per year when the discount rate is 5%?

a. $3,000,000

b. $7,500,000

c. $30,000

d. none of the above

23. You have a credit card that is charging you a nominal rate of 22% annually. What is the effective annual rate that you will really end up being charged per year?

a. $1 - (0.0183)^{12} + 1$

b. $1 + (0.0183)^{12} - 1$

c. $(0.0183)^{12} - 1$

d. $1 + (0.0183)^{6} - 1$

e. none of the above

24. You are expecting cash inflows of $100, $300, $600, $900, and $1,200 respectively, over the next 5 years. The interest rate is 7%. What is the future value of this series of cash flows?

a. $3,468.40

b. $217.00

c. $3,100.00

d. $3,348.60

25. The probability of a boom economy is 30%, the probability of a normal economy is 50%, and the probability of a recession is 20%. Do-Nuts Co. has predicted that the return on its stock will be 15% in a boom economy, 8% in a normal economy, and 0% in a recession. What is the expected rate of return for Do-Nuts Co.?

a. 6.5%

b. 8.5%

c. 8.0%

d. 6.0%

26. An increase in the rate of inflation causes the security market line to:

a. increase in slope

b. shift downward

c. shift upward

d. stay the same

TEST YOURSELF

27. An increase in the risk aversion of investors causes the security market line to:

a. increase in slope

b. decrease in slope

c. shift upward

d. stay the same

28. A yield curve is considered normal when it shows that:

a. short-term interest rates are greater than long-term interest rates

b. long-term interest rates are greater than short-term interest rates

c. long- and short-term interest rates are equal

d. none of the above

29. When calculating future value with semiannual compounding, what do you need to do to use the FVIF table?

a. divide the interest rate by 2 and multiply the number of periods by 2

b. multiply the interest rate by 2 and divide the number of periods by 2

c. keep interest rates and number of periods the same but multiply the final value by 2

d. use the same interest rate but divide the number of periods by 2

30. Your portfolio currently consists of Stock A, which has a beta of 1.2 and makes up 40% of your portfolio. 35% of your portfolio consists of Stock B, with a beta of 0.85; and the remaining 25% of your portfolio is made up of Stock C, which has a beta of 1.4. You consider adding a new stock to your existing portfolio, but you are extremely risk averse and fear that the addition of the new stock could increase your risk. The new stock, Stock D, has a beta of 1.4. If you purchase the new stock you will have to sell 10% of Stock A, and then Stock D would make up 10% of your new portfolio. Should you add the new stock? Why or why not?

End in sweet fishtail into monster-truck of shame.
— Lotion

31. You have won a radio contest. You can receive either $500,000 in cash today or a 10-year annuity that has a 6% interest rate and annual payments of $60,000. Which prize should you choose and why?

32. Boogerglue Corporation has a beta of 1.9. You are interested in investing in Boogerglue Corporation because you have read that its product is the new wave in envelope sealants. But the financial magazines say that the current expected return on Boogerglue's stock is 8% and you just aren't sure if that is a good deal because, although you like the product, you don't like too much risk. The current rate on a T-bill is 7% and the current average stock market return is 10%. What is your required rate of return on Boogerglue? Should you invest in Boogerglue stock? Why?

TEST YOURSELF

33. The economy is in pretty good shape. There is a 20% chance of a boom occurring, a 70% chance of a normal economy, and only a 10% chance of the economy slipping into a recession. You own stock in a company called Fishface, Inc. In a normal economy, Fishface's return is 20%, but in a boom it shoots up to 80% and in a recession it drops to 215%.

a. What is the expected rate of return for Fishface stock?

b. What is the standard deviation of Fishface stock?

c. What is Fishface's coefficient of variation?

34. You could take your money out of Fishface and invest it in a new company called Dog Chew. In a boom economy, Dog Chew will provide a return of 70%. In a normal economy, its return is projected to be 30%. In a recession, the return will be 5%.

a. What is the expected rate of return for Dog Chew's stock?

b. Using the information from question 33, plot Fishface's and Dog Chew's returns on a probability distribution.

c. Which stock has a more pointed probability distribution?

d. Therefore, which stock is a safer investment for a risk averse investor like you?

0:36:55

Stock and Bond Valuation

A **stock** is a security that pays its owner dividends and represents part ownership of a corporation. There are two classifications of stock: common and preferred.

A **bond** is a loan. The borrowing company agrees to pay the bondholder (lender) interest for a given period for the use of his or her money and then at a set date, repays the loan in full.

0:38:28

Section A: Terms

Par value is the face-value of a bond. It is the amount of money that the company borrows from an investor and promises to repay at a specific date in the future. Typically, the par value of a bond is $1,000.

Coupon payments are the dollar installments of interest that the borrowing company pays to the investor each period that the bond is held. Coupon payments typically occur every six months, but can also be paid annually.

The **coupon interest rate** is the annual rate of interest on a bond. The coupon interest rate is calculated by dividing the coupon payment by the par value of the bond. A bond's coupon interest rate is always stated in its indenture.

The contract that the borrowing company writes, which states the details of the bond, is known as the **indenture**.

V2

VIDEO NOTES

The interest rate on new bonds is the **market interest rate**. The market interest rate is affected by changes in the market as a whole, and therefore changes daily. When calculating the present value of bonds, the market interest rate is used to determine the present value interest factor.

A bond's **maturity date** is the specified date on which the par value must be repaid.

Forgetaboutit.
— Johnny Depp, ***Donnie Brasco***

0:48:05

Section B: Bond Present Value

Almost all bonds have coupon payments that are paid over a specific period of time. A bond's coupon payments are similar to annuity payments because they represent a constant, steady stream of payments made to the investor over a specific period of time. Therefore, when calculating the present value of a bond, the present value interest factor of an annuity (PVIFA) can be used to determine the present value of the coupon payments.

STANDARD DEVIANT FINANCIAL INFO:

Investors calculate the present value of a bond to determine the current fair price for that bond.

Once the present value of the coupon payments has been determined, the present value of the par value of the bond can be added to the coupon payment's present value to determine the entire present value of the bond. Because the par value of a bond is a lump-sum payment made to the investor at maturity, its present value is calculated using the present value interest factor (PVIF).

Therefore, **bond present value** (BPV) is:

BPV = (coupon payment) [PVIFA(market rate, remaining periods)] + (par value)[PVIF(market rate, remaining periods)]

V2

VIDEO NOTES

When using the bond present value formula, it is important to remember that the interest rate used is the market interest rate, and the number of periods equals the number of periods remaining until the bond's maturity.

Let's say Joe Investor is selling a Mandu-Cook bond. Mandu-Cook is an unusual Thai restaurant and mambo room. Its bond carries an 8% coupon rate, a $1,000 par value at a maturity in 10 years, and has annual coupon payments. Of course, before you rush out to buy the bond, you want to figure out what it's worth to you. First, you run out to read the *Wall Street Journal* to get the market interest rate on a similar bond, which is 10%. Just plug the numbers into the bond valuation formulas we just discussed.

First set up your equation. The present value of the bond, or BPV, equals the annual payment (or $80) times the PVIFA plus the par value (or $1,000) times the PVIF:

$$\textbf{BPV} = \textbf{80 [PVIFA(\%,n)] + 1,000 [PVIF(\%,n)]}$$

Now, refer to your present value tables and plug in the figures you need. The PVIFA for 10 periods at 10% is 6.1446. And the PVIF for 10 periods at 10% is 0.3855.

So, the present value of our bond is equal to the $80 yearly payment times 6.1446 plus the $1,000 par value of the bond times 0.3855:

$$\textbf{BPV} = \textbf{80 (6.1446) + 1000 (0.3855)}$$

This arithmetic comes out to 877.07.

$$BPV = 491.57 + 385.50$$

$$BPV = 877.07$$

Now if we were to shake things up a little, and say there were only 8 years left until maturity, instead of 10, what would you do?

The same calculation you just did. Just reduce the number of periods from 10 to 8 when you're looking at the PVIF and PVIFA tables.

Section C: Discount and Premium Bonds

0:54:40

Coupon rates of bonds are fixed, but market interest rates are not the most stable things. Market interest rates move up and down all the time. So, when market interest rates rise, the value of a bond decreases. Why? Since the coupon rate on a bond is fixed, a person holding a bond at an old, small interest rate receives less money from interest than someone who bought a newly issued, higher interest bond today, because the new bond has the new higher interest rate.

When market interest rates rise, bondholders will typically choose to sell their low interest bonds and purchase new higher interest bonds. However, because the market rate is higher than the investor's outstanding bond, the investor will need to sell the bond at a discount.

A **discount bond** is one that sells below its par value because the going rate of interest is greater than the bond's coupon payment.

When investors choose to sell a bond at a discount, they need to compute the size of the discount on the existing bond to determine the appropriate selling price.

To compute the size of discount needed on an existing bond when market interest rates have increased, subtract the

coupon payment on a new bond from the coupon payment on your existing bond and then multiply that negative number by the PVIFA for the remaining number of periods and the new market interest rate.

Discount = (old payment − new payment) x [PVIFA (new rate and periods)]

Let's look at a brief example:

You bought a $1,000 Mandu-Cook bond. There are eight years left until maturity. When you bought the bond, it had an 8% coupon rate and an $80 coupon payment. Interest rates have since increased to 10%. If you bought the same bond in the market today you would receive a $100 coupon payment.

For you to sell your crummy, low-interest bond today, you need to discount it to compete with the newer bonds on the market that have the 10% rate. How much should you discount your bond to sell it? Easy. As we told you, just plug in the numbers.

To compute the discount, we subtract the new coupon payment from the old coupon payment, then apply the PVIFA.

Discount = 80 −100 [PVIFA(10%, 8 periods)]

Subtract 100 (the coupon payment on a new bond) from 80 (the coupon payment on your bond), and multiply this amount by the PVIFA for the new rate, 10%, and 8 time periods. And you know how to do that, just look at your present value tables.

$$\text{Discount} = (80 - 100)[\text{PVIFA}(10\%,8)]$$
$$= -20\ (5.3349)$$
$$= -106.70$$

So, then you multiply −20 times 5.3349 and get −106.70. $106.70 is the amount that you need to discount your bond.

$$1{,}000 - 106.70 = 893.30$$

So, you take the par value of your bond, which is $1,000, and subtract the discount, $106.70 to get $893.30. You will need to sell your outstanding bond for $893.30.

Because interest rates fluctuate both up and down, the market interest rate is just as likely to decrease while an investor holds an existing bond with a higher coupon rate. If market interest rates decline, an existing bond with a higher coupon rate will be worth more than par value and its holder can sell it at a premium.

A **premium bond** is one that sells above its par value because the going rate of interest falls below the bond's coupon rate.

To calculate the premium that should be added to the par value of a bond if interest rates have decreased, simply sub-

tract the coupon payment on a new bond from the coupon payment on the existing bond and then multiply that positive number by the PVIFA for the remaining number of periods and the new market interest rate.

Premium = (old payment − new payment) × [PVIFA (new rate, remaining periods)]

Once the premium has been calculated, it must be added to the par value of the existing bond. The sum of the premium and the bond's par value is the price for which the existing bond should be sold.

Current Yield

Another important concept to understand when dealing with bonds is **yield**. Yield is essentially a rate of return that is earned on an investment.

Specifically, yield is the rate of return that an investor is most concerned with because it is based on the value of the investment rather than on the par value of a bond.

The **current yield** on a bond is calculated by dividing the annual interest payment of a bond by the bond's current price.

$$\textbf{Current yield} = \frac{\textbf{annual interest/coupon payment}}{\textbf{Current price}}$$

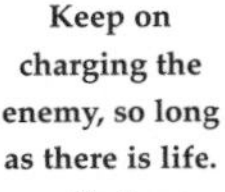

Keep on charging the enemy, so long as there is life.
— Fortune cookie

Simple enough, but let's do an example:

Looking in the paper, we find that a bond from Best Buy® is selling for $925. The current payment is $85 per period.

$$\frac{85}{925} = 0.919 = 9.19\%$$

So let's divide that quickly. 85 divided by 925 is 9.19%, which, coincidentally, is the current yield listed in the newspaper.

Because yield is calculated using the current price of a bond as opposed to the bond's par value, it is a more accurate measure of the rate of return that an investor will earn if he or she purchases a bond at a given price. However, since original investors often do not hold bonds until maturity, bond investors tend to calculate a bond's **yield to maturity** and the bond's **yield to call** more frequently than current yield.

Yield to Maturity

Yield to maturity (YTM) is the rate of return earned on a bond if it is held to maturity. Calculating a bond's yield to maturity is a tedious process. To calculate yield to maturity, the pre-

sent value of a bond equation needs to be solved for the interest rate (i). Unfortunately, the only way to accurately solve for i is through trial and error.

Or, like they do in the video, you can use a financial calculator.

To calculate a bond's yield to maturity using a financial calculator, simply enter the number of periods (n), the bond's current price (PV), which is a negative number, then enter the coupon payment (PMT) and the par value of the bond at maturity (FV). Then press the i (interest rate) key. The yield to maturity appears and you've got your answer.

Here, let's try one. Let's say we have 12 years left on our $1,000 par value bond. It has a coupon payment of $90, and is trading for $1,100. Just stick those buggers into the calculator.

12 n

1,100 +/- PV

90 PMT

1000 FV

Compute i

The yield to maturity of this guy is 7.69%.

Yield to Call

Yield to call (YTC) is the rate of return on a bond if it is called before it matures. If the business or organization that issued the bond placed call provisions on the bond, it has reserved the right to buy the bond back from the investor before its maturity date. Organizations typically place call provisions on their bonds to avoid losing money on interest payments because of unpredictable interest rate fluctuations over time.

A call provision on a bond is typically part of the bond's indenture, and states that the issuing organization must pay the bondholder an amount greater than the par value if the bond is called. This additional sum is known as a **call premium**. Therefore, when calculating a bond's yield to call, the call premium needs to be included in the call price, or future value.

STUDY SIDEKICK

Calculating yield to call without a financial calculator is a tedious process of trial and error. However, when you use a financial calculator, calculating yield to call on a particular bond is a simple process.

To calculate a bond's yield to call using a financial calculator, enter the number of years until the company can call the bond (n), then enter the current price of the bond (PV), then enter the coupon payment on the bond (PMT), and finally the call price (FV), which is the par value of the bond plus the call premium. Press i, the interest rate key. Then the yield to call, which is your answer, appears.

Let's try yield to call on a bond. We'll say this bond has 6 years until it can be called. It's trading for $1,200 today. The coupon payment is $80, and the call premium is 4%. So the future par value of the bond is $1,040.

Your lucky numbers are 3, 7, 15, 19, 41, 50

— A different fortune cookie

Enter:

6 n

1200 +/- PV

80 PMT

1040 FV

Compute i

After a few seconds, that returns the yield to call of 4.69%.

SUMMARY

- $ Bonds have a value based on the stream of payments from their coupon interest rate, or interest payments; and their par value, or face-value.
- $ As market interest rates change, so does the value of an outstanding bond; as interest rates go up, the value of a bond goes down, and vice versa.
- $ Bonds are also described by their yields.
- $ Current yield equals the annual coupon interest rate divided by the current price of the bond.
- $ Yield to maturity is the return on the bond from the current date until the bond matures.
- $ Yield to call is calculated based on the repayment of par value by the company before the bond is mature.

0:58:25

Section D: Stock Valuation

Preferred Stock

Preferred stock is a security with a fixed, permanent dividend for as long as the investor owns the stock. Preferred stock is essentially a cross between common stock and bonds. Preferred stockholders do not have voting rights in the company.

STANDARD DEVIANT FINANCIAL INFO:

Not all preferred stocks last forever. Some have specific maturity dates. These are pretty rare, though.

Irrational enthusiasm is a valuable commodity.
— Carolyn Hax, The Washington Post

To calculate the present value of preferred stock, use the perpetuity equation, substituting the stock dividend in for the perpetuity payment:

$$\text{PV of preferred stock} = \frac{\text{dividend}}{\text{discount rate}}$$

If the current selling price, or present value, of the preferred stock is known, you can use a different form of the same equation to calculate the rate of return on the stock:

$$\text{Rate of return } (K_p) = \frac{\text{dividend}}{\text{PV}}$$

Common Stock

Common stock is part ownership in a company. The company can pay you dividends, but it doesn't have to. If the company makes a profit, it can pay out the dividends or retain the earn-

ings to do stuff. If you were a bondholder, the company would simply owe you money (because bonds are debt), but the company has to make interest payments every period. Just like you, a company has to make its loan payments.

The company has the freedom to decide the amount of dividend paid to its common stock holders. Therefore, common stock is riskier than bonds or preferred stock. But, greater risk means greater chance for bigger returns. The price of a stock depends on the market and the company's success.

The value of a common stock is based on two components: the value of its dividends and the expected increase in the stock's market value.

If an investor decides to sell his or her common stock and the price of that stock has increased since its purchase, the investor will realize a capital gain. If, however, the investor is forced to sell the stock for less than its original purchase price, the investor will experience a capital loss.

You might be thinking, "Hey, if I'm a stockholder, I want those dividends!" The thing is, if the company retains its earnings, you may not get more cash, but the value of the stock itself should rise, because the company retained those earnings so it could grow. For our purposes, a rise in stock price is just as good as a dividend.

Even with the volatility of the market, common stock valuation is still important. We need to know what to expect from a stock, and therefore, what a fair price would be for that stock.

STUDY SIDEKICK

To calculate the present value of common stock, we use a variation of the equation used to determine the present value of a bond. The main difference in valuing stock is that instead of using the fixed payment for bonds, or PAY, you use the potential dividend for the stock, or DIV.

PV of common stock =

$$\frac{DIV_1}{(1 + K_s)^1} + \frac{DIV_2}{(1 + K_s)^2} + \frac{DIV_3}{(1 + K_s)^3} + \text{...to infinity...} + \frac{Price}{(1 + K)^n}$$

Because companies are assumed to last forever, the dividends on their stock are also assumed to last to infinity, which makes this formula for determining stock's present value complicated.

The **constant growth model** (also referred to as the **Gordon growth model**) is typically used to value common stock. The constant growth equation uses present value and the dividend to determine a fair price for a given stock.

VIDEO NOTES

V2

The constant growth model sets the price (P_0) equal to the dividend in time one (D_1) over the rate of return (K_s) minus the growth rate (g).

$$P_0 = \frac{D_1}{(K_s - g)}$$

To determine the time dividend, or expected dividend payment (D_1), set it equal to the current dividend (D_0) multiplied by one plus the growth rate (g).

$$D_1 = D_0\,(1 + g)$$

So we need to use the Gordon growth model to decide how much to pay for Pizza Coli's stock.

Dividend:	$D_0 = 2$
Growth:	$g = 0.10$
Rate of return:	$K_s = 0.14$

Study Sidekick

Pizza Coli's last annual dividend was $2, and you expect the dividend to grow at a rate of 10% (your growth rate). You also expect a 14% rate of return for the stock. That means 14 is your K_s, or rate of return.

$$\begin{aligned} D_1 &= D_0\,(1 + g) \\ &= 2\,(1 + 0.10) \\ &= 2.20 \end{aligned}$$

The stock's "time one" dividend is equal to the current dividend, D_0, multiplied by the quantity of one plus the growth rate, g. 2, the current dividend, times the quantity of 1 plus 0.10 equals $2.20.

Okay, so now we have the dividend for time one. We remember from before that the expected rate of return for this stock is 14%, and the growth rate is ten percent.

To find the current price of the stock, P_0, the Gordon growth model says to put the final dividend, D_1, over the rate of return, K_s, minus the growth rate, g.

$$\begin{aligned} P_0 &= \frac{2.20}{0.14 - 0.10} \\ &= \frac{2.20}{0.04} \\ &= 55.00 \end{aligned}$$

So that's 2.2 over 0.14 minus 0.10. That reduces to 2.2 over 0.04, which equals 55.00.

Pizza Coli's stock is worth $55.

Stock prices and dividends have an incestuous relationship. Every stock's value is based on its market price and dividends. But the market price is also based on the dividends. Whether you're determining the expected value of a stock or its future selling price, dividends play a critical role.

If a company's dividends grow regularly over time, its stock is referred to as a **constant growth stock**. Constant growth means that the dividends of the company increase at the same rate over time.

In general, growth stocks are much more valuable than non-growth stocks.

Differential or Supernormal Growth Stock

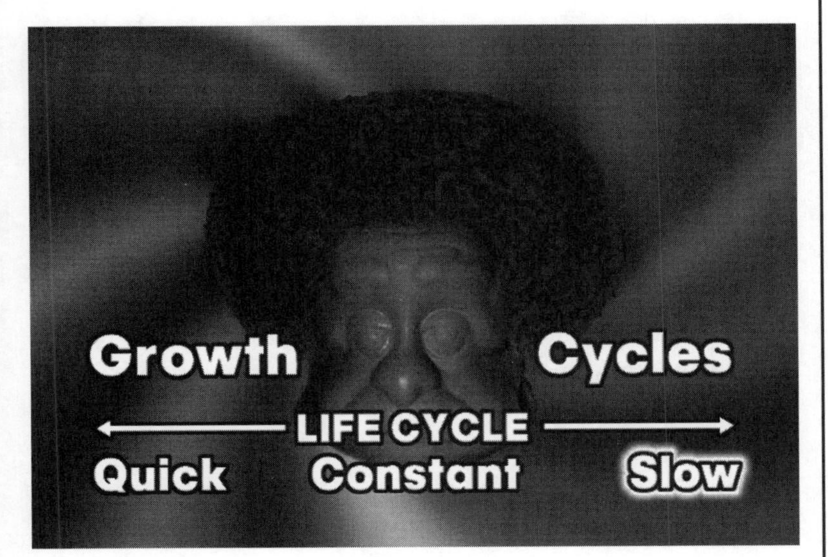

STUDY SIDEKICK

Most companies experience **growth cycles** during their life span. They typically experience rapid growth early in their life, followed by a constant growth rate and finally, toward the end of their life cycle, growth slows significantly. This pattern of growth is known as nonconstant growth.

Unfortunately, there is no specific equation for estimating the value of a stock growing at uneven rates, so you need to follow four main steps that include the use of the constant growth formula to determine the value of supernormal growth stocks.

The formula for valuing supernormal growth stocks consists of four major steps:

1. Calculate the present value of the dividends during the supernormal period.

2. Apply the constant growth formula to determine the stock value at the *end* of the high growth period. (Note: The value of the stock at the end of the high growth period is the same as the stock's value at the *beginning* of the normal growth period or, time n.) Use the stock's first dividend once it returns to normal growth for D_{n+1}, use the required rate of return for K_s, and use the constant growth rate for g.

3. Discount the value of the stock to present day prices using the present value interest factor (PVIF). (Use the PVIF based on the number of years the stock took to return to normal growth and the current market discount rate.)
4. Discount the dividends from the supernormal periods and add them to the present value of the stock determined in step 3.

V2

Video Notes

Again, let's learn through an example using our hypothetical company. When Pizza Coli first comes into existence, its stock has a growth rate of 20% per year. Then things settled down after 2 years and moved more normally and sustainably at 7%. For an investor, we'll say that the required rate of return is 10%. The last dividend was $2. How do you figure out the present value or price of the stock?

Step 1

First you need to establish the value of the dividends over the first three years. Why three instead of two? Because we need that dividend to use in the normal growth formula in step 2.

Year 0: $2.00

So you begin with a $2 dividend in year 0. With 20% growth, the dividend in year 1 grows to $2.40. That's $2 plus another 20%, right?

20% growth

Year 1: $2.40

Again, with 20% growth, the dividend in year 2 is valued at $2.88.

20% growth

Year 2: $2.88

Okay, now growth returns to normal, the first dividend of the normal period. Take the year 2 dividend and multiply it by one plus the normal growth rate, so that's 1.07 times 2.88, totaling a $3.08 dividend.

7% growth

Year 3: $3.08

Step 2

Now step 2. Stick the year 3 dividend into the constant growth formula, using the constant growth rate for g. So the price equals the year 3 dividend, 3.08, over 0.10, the required rate of return, minus 0.07, the growth rate.

$$\frac{3.08}{0.10 - 0.07} = 102.67$$

COMPUTE! 102.67

This price is the value of the stock based on the dividend of period three (or at the end of year 2).

Step 3

Now we move on to step 3: discount the value of the stock to present-day prices using the present value interest factor.

$$\textbf{PV of stock} = \textbf{102.67[PVIF(10\%, 2)]}$$

$$= \textbf{102.67(0.8265)}$$

$$= \textbf{84.86}$$

We use the PVIF we find at the intersection of 2, for the two years, and 10%, for the current discount rate. The value of the stock,102.67, times the PVIF for 10% and two periods is 102.67 times 0.8265—which equals 84.86

Step 4

Discount each dividend in the supernormal growth period. Looking at your PVIF table, find each dividend's PVIF based on the period that the dividend came from and the required rate of return, which is 10%. Then multiply each dividend by its corresponding PVIF.

$$\mathbf{D_1 = 2.40[PVIF(10\%,1)]}$$

$$\mathbf{D_1 = 2.40(0.9091)}$$

$$\mathbf{D_1 = 2.18}$$

The dividend of year 1 is \$2.40 times the PVIF of 10% and one period, or 0.9091. Compute that and it equals \$2.18.

$$D_2 = 2.88[PVIF(10\%,1)]$$

$$D_2 = 2.88(0.8264)$$

$$D_2 = 2.38$$

The dividend of year 2 is \$2.88 times the PVIF of 10% and two periods, or 0.8264. Compute that and it equals \$2.38.

Now, we'll add these numbers to the present value of the constant growth to come up with the total present value of Pizza Coli's supernormal stock.

$$2.18 + 2.38 + 84.86 = 89.42$$

Graphically Stunning! — Lew Simms

The present value of dividend 1, plus the present value of dividend 2, plus the present value of the dividends during normal growth equals 89.42. We have determined that the total present value of this supernormal stock is $89.42.

SUMMARY

- **The present value of a bond is determined by adding the PVIFA of its coupon payments to the PVIF of the bond's final sale value.**
- **Stocks, on the other hand, are easy as long as their dividends are growing at a constant rate; then you can just use the constant growth model.**
- **If the stocks have irregular or differential growth, then you have to figure the present value of individual dividends, and when the stocks go back to normal growth, you can use the constant growth model again.**

Quiz 5

1. A _______________ is a security that provides the investor with part ownership in a corporation and pays a dividend.

2. A bond is a ___________________ to a company by an investor.

3. The amount of money that a business borrows and promises to repay at a specific future date is the ______________. It is also the face value of a bond.

4. Par value is typically $___________.

5. The annual rate of interest on a bond is the ____________________________. It is calculated by __________________ the coupon payment by the par value.

6. The __________________________ rate is the rate of interest being offered on new bonds today.

7. The specified date on which the par value of a bond must be repaid is the bond's ____________________________.

QUIZ

8. To easily compute the present value of a bond, you can treat the coupon payments like a ____________________.

9. The formula used to calculate bond present value is ____.

10. When looking at the present value tables and working with bonds, it is important to remember that the interest rate you should be using is the ____________________, and the number of periods equals the ________________________.

11. When market interest rates rise, the value of a bond ____________________.

12. A bond that sells below its par value because the market interest rate is higher than its coupon rate is called a ______________________ bond.

13. The formula used to calculate the size of a discount on an existing bond when interest rates have increased is ____.

14. A bond that sells above its par value is a ______________.

15. Interest rates and bond prices have a(n) ________________ relationship—as interest rates increase, bond prices ____________________.

16. ______________________ on a bond is calculated by dividing the annual interest payment by the bond's current price.

17. ______________________ is the rate of return earned on a bond if it is held to maturity.

18. To calculate a bond's yield to maturity, you solve the bond present value equation for i (the interest rate). To do this on a financial calculator you simply enter the following: ____.

19. ____________________ is the rate of return on a bond if the issuing company calls it before it reaches maturity.

20. The main reason that a business would exercise its right to call in a bond is if ____________________________________.

21. The money above and beyond the bond's par value that a business would be required to pay an investor if his or her bond was called is known as the ______________________.

Quiz

22. __________________________ is like a cross between a bond and common stock.

23. __________________________ represents a piece of ownership in a company and entitles its holder to dividends.

24. The equation used to calculate the present value of a preferred stock is __________________________________.

25. The formula used to calculate the rate of return on a preferred stock (K_p) is __________________________________.

26. Investors realize a __________________________ when stock that they hold is sold and the price of it has increased since its purchase.

27. If an investor sells a stock at a price lower than what he or she paid for it, the investor realizes a

________________________________.

28. The constant growth model for valuing stocks, also known as the __________________________ model, is

________________________________.

29. The formula used to calculate the final dividend (D_1) portion of the constant growth model is

______________________________.

30. A stock's value consists of its _________________________ and its ____________________.

31. Companies go through growth cycles. Typically they grow ________________ early in their lifespan, then they grow ____________________________, and finally at the end of their life cycle their growth is _____________ than the economy.

Whee!!!
— Snail, riding on a turtle's back.

32. When a company's stock is growing faster than the economy, at an unsustainable rate, it is considered to be experiencing __________________________ growth.

33. There is no easy formula for calculating the value of supernormal growth stocks. So, we follow several steps. The first step is to figure out the present value of

_________________________. The second step is to

______________________________________. Then you discount the value of the stock to present-day values using the

_____________. Finally, we discount __________________ from the supernormal periods and add them to the

______________________________.

Quiz

34. You can find PVIF and FVIF values on

____________________________.

35. As long as stock is growing at a constant rate you can use the ____________________________ to determine their value. However, if a stock has an irregular growth pattern, you have to figure the present value of individual __________________ and then, when the stock's growth goes back to normal, use the

___________________________________.

STUDY SIDEKICK

A Brief Work of Historical Fiction

Cerebellum Corporation: The Rise of a Dragon

Cerebellum Corporation opened its doors on February 16, 1967. The original offices were in Arlington, Virginia, and the company employed six people.

Cerebellum was created as a front for an insidious underground crime organization known only as The Jive Poppies. No one was safe from the Jive Poppies. Up and down the Atlantic coast, federal agents learned to fear their name. The Jive Poppies' reign of terror lasted seven years.

In 1974, an international conglomerate named GlobeCo bought Cerebellum and The Jive Poppies. All seemed calm as Cerebellum employees shifted their activities from money laundering to legitimate enterprise.

The Rise of a Dragon

The business started small, with a small foray into coaster production, and then Cerebellum moved into car sales and real estate. Business was booming, and the cash rolled in. Some employees balked at the prospect of actually performing labor in exchange for a paycheck, but newer, younger go-getters soon replaced them.

GlobeCo began to take more control of Cerebellum as GlobeCo began its gambit for world domination in 1982. Two platoons of shock troops were based at Cerebellum to prepare for the invasion of Washington. Surprise was essential, and GlobeCo had hoped that world attention would be riveted by the Falklands War. It wasn't. GlobeCo's subversion ended in the bloody Battle of Arlington Boulevard. At the battle, both platoons of GlobeCo shock troops and five Cerebellum employees received a sound head-thumping from a detachment of grapefruit-wielding U.S. Army Rangers.

By 1983, Cerebellum was again an independent company, and moved its offices to McLean, Virginia.

No Cerebellum employees can remember what they did between 1983 and 1995, but they are reasonably sure it was fun. Upon becoming more conscious in March 1995, Cerebellum employees were puzzled to find the floors of the office covered with Blatz cans and empty tubs of mayonnaise.

"It's kind of a blur," said one employee. "But I remember hearing a lot of Cuban music and watching someone carry my pants around on a ten-foot pole."

Starting in late 1995, Cerebellum started producing Video Course Reviews, and it has done so ever since.

STUDY SIDEKICK

VIDEO TIME CODE

The Wild and Wacky World of Finance Part 3

0:03:43 .... **I. Review**

0:09:00 .... **II. Cost of capital**

A. The logic of cost of capital

0:09:23 .... 1. Cost of capital

0:10:20 .... 2. Capital components

0:11:47 .... 3. Capital structure

0:11:57 .... 4. Weighted average cost of capital

0:15:30 .... B. Cost of debt

0:15:38 .... 1. Calculating cost of debt

0:16:56 .... 2. Example

0:17:56 .... C. Cost of preferred stock

0:18:04 .... 1. Calculating cost of preferred stock

0:18:36 .... 2. Example

0:19:45 .... D. Cost of retained earnings

0:22:00 .... 1. CAPM

0:23:55 .... 2. Bond-Yield-Plus-Risk-Premium

Topic	Time
3. Discounted cash flow	0:25:16
E. Cost of issuing new common stock	0:27:40
F. Calculating the weighted average cost of capital	0:30:56
1. WACC when using retained earnings	0:32:20
2. WACC when issuing new common stock	0:34:40
G. Marginal cost of capital	0:36:10
III. Basics of capital budgeting	0:38:38
A. What is capital budgeting?	0:38:45
1. Definition	0:39:00
2. Where do projects come from?	0:40:25
B. Different kinds of projects	0:41:14
1. Mandatory projects	0:41:30
2. Expansion projects	0:41:55
3. Replacement projects	0:42:08
C. Isn't this similar to stock valuation?	0:43:34
D. Capital budgeting decision methods	0:46:06
1. Payback	0:47:28
2. Discounted payback	0:52:18
3. Net present value	0:56:20
4. Profitability index	1:01:00
5. Internal Rate of Return (IRR)	1:02:58
6. Modified Internal Rate of Return (MIRR)	1:07:44

1:14:14 .... **IV. Capital budgeting with certainty**

1:14:20 .... A. What are we doing?

1:15:00 .... 1. Cash flows

1:15:13 .... 2. Incremental cash flows

1:15:29 .... 3. The game plan

1:15:50 .... 4. Captain Blahr

1:16:50 .... B. Cash flows and the process

1:17:22 .... 1. Net investment cash outlay

a. New equipment

b. Change in net working capital

1:18:26 .... 2. Operating cash flows (OCFs)

a. Total income

b. Total costs

c. Subtract depreciation

d. Subtract taxes

e. Add back depreciation

1:20:12 .... 3. Net disposal cash flow

a. Salvage value

b. Subtract taxes

c. Return on net working capital

C. Evaluation of a capital budget 1:29:18

1. Payback 1:29:30
2. Discounted payback 1:30:28
3. Net present value 1:31:26
4. Profitability index 1:31:58
5. IRR 1:32:39
6. MIRR 1:33:17

D. Capital budgeting for replacement 1:35:10

1. Intro to Z-Co and replacement 1:35:15
2. NICO 1:38:57
3. Changes to OCFs 1:40:28
    a. After-tax savings on expenses
    b. After-tax benefits on depreciation
4. Net disposal cash flow 1:44:22
5. Finding the present value 1:45:54
6. Evaluation 1:46:59

VIDEO NOTES

The Wild and Wacky World of Finance Part 3

Cost of Capital, Capital Budgeting, and Cookies

Mirth is the key to unopened doors. Read a book!
— A third fortune cookie

0:03:43

Review

This part of the video was all review. If it doesn't seem that familiar to you, flip back through the Study Sidekick.

V3

VIDEO NOTES

The Logic of the Cost of Capital

0:09:00

Section A: Cost of Capital

The **cost of capital** is a capital budgeting concept that describes the cost of raising money (capital). Businesses continually need more money to invest, purchase equipment, acquire other businesses, or any other activity that involves money. Businesses use stocks, bonds, preferred stock, and retained earnings to raise the capital (money) required to initiate a capital project.

However, raising new capital costs businesses. Businesses incur costs for printing stock certificates, paying interest to bondholders, paying dividends to stockholders and all kinds of other stuff (like cookies). The cost of capital measures the amount of money that a business has to spend to raise more money. In other words, the cost of capital is the percentage of every dollar that a business raises that goes back to pay for the

the costs of raising that same dollar. For instance, a cost of capital of 10% means that every dollar in capital that a business raises costs it 10 cents.

Capital Components

The instruments that a business uses to raise capital, known as **capital components**, consist of common stock, preferred stock, bonds, and retained earnings.

STANDARD DEVIANT FINANCIAL INFO:

Bonds are often referred to simply as debt. Common stock and retained earnings are often grouped together and referred to collectively as common equity or simply "equity."

Each capital component has its own cost of capital. We refer to these as the cost of debt, the cost of retained earnings, the cost of common stock, and the cost of preferred stock.

Most companies need to estimate the cost of capital for each of the capital components because when they raise capital, they use a combination of all of the capital components.

The specific way in which businesses choose to organize their capital components to raise capital is known as their **capital structure**. The proportion of each capital component that a business chooses to use when raising capital is referred to as the **weight** of the component. (Example: if a company raises 30% capital through bonds, its weight of debt is 30%.)

Weighted Average Cost of Capital

A business's cost of capital when combining the specific weights of each capital component together is called the **weighted average cost of capital (WACC)**. To calculate a business's WACC, multiply each capital component's cost of capital by its weight and then add them all together.

SUMMARY

- ¢ **The cost of capital is a percentage that represents how much of every dollar that needs to be spent to get the same dollar.**
- ¢ **Common stocks, preferred stocks, bonds, and retained earnings are called capital components.**
- ¢ **Each capital component has its own cost of capital.**
- ¢ **Businesses tend to use all the components at the same time to raise capital, in proportions that create the capital structure.**
- ¢ **To find the overall cost of capital, we have to multiply each capital component's cost of capital by its proportion and then add them together. This overall cost of capital is called the weighted average cost of capital or WACC.**

0:15:30

Section B: Cost of Debt

The cost of debt is the cost of issuing bonds. In calculating the weighted average cost of capital for an organization, the **after-tax cost of debt** is used.

The government gives businesses a tax break for incurring debt, by making it tax deductible. Therefore, it is important to use the cost of debt as the market interest rate of the debt, minus the tax savings that result because interest is deductible.

The formula used to calculate the cost of debt is the interest rate on debt (K_d), times the quantity of 1 minus the tax rate $(1 - T)$.

$$\textbf{Cost of debt} = K_d(1 - T)$$

VIDEO NOTES

Cynical Coffee Company, or CCC, caters to the disenchanted souls of several generations. CCC's lack of distinct service and its dirty-looking customers have made the company a big hit. Cynical Coffee Company decides to take out a bond to do some expansion.

Let's say that the Cynical Coffee Company can borrow debt at an interest rate of 9% and it has an income tax rate of 30%.

$$\begin{aligned} K_d(1 - T) &= 0.09\ (120.30) \\ &= 0.09\ (0.70) \\ &= 0.063 \end{aligned}$$

Its after-tax cost of debt is calculated as 9%, the interest rate on the bonds, times the quantity of 1 minus 0.30, the tax rate. Or, 0.09 times 0.70, which equals 0.063. So, CCC's after-tax cost of debt is 6.3%.

0:17:56

Section C: Cost of Preferred Stock

In calculating the WACC, the second item needed is the **cost of preferred stock**. The cost of preferred stock (K_{ps}) is equal to the dividend (D_{ps}), divided by the net issuing price (P_p), which is the price per share that the company receives after deducting **underwriting costs**.

$$K_{ps} = \frac{D_{ps}}{P_p}$$

Let's assume that Cynical Coffee Company has preferred stock that pays a $10 dividend per share and sells for $100 per share.

Whenever Cynical Coffee Company issues new preferred stock shares, it incurs an underwriting charge of 3% or $3 per share. So CCC makes, or nets, only $97 per share.

$$K_{ps} = \frac{10}{97}$$
$$= 0.103$$

The cost of preferred stock, K_{ps}, equals $10, the dividend, or D, divided by $97, the net issuing price, or P_p. That equals 0.103. So, the cost of issuing preferred stock for CCC is 10.3%.

STUDY SIDEKICK

0:19:45

Section D: Cost of Retained Earnings

The third portion needed when calculating a business' WACC is the **cost of retained earnings**. A company's cost of retained earnings is equal to its stockholders' required rate of return.

When a business makes a profit, it is required to pay its interest and preferred stock dividends. However, whatever money remains once the business has done so can either be paid out to the common stockholders as dividends or placed in retained earnings.

You can't stomp a snake with two feet in a bucket.
— H. Ross Perot

If the company decides to retain the earnings, its stockholders will demand that they use the fund. The use of the retained earnings must increase the stockholders' earnings per share just as much as if the stockholders had received the dividends and reinvested them into the same company.

There are three approaches to determining the cost of retained earnings. They are the **capital asset pricing model (CAPM), the bond-yield-plus-risk-premium approach,** and **the discounted cash flow approach (DCA).**

CAPM

The **capital asset pricing model (CAPM)** is a formula that uses an estimate of the risk-free rate (K_{rf}), the stock's beta coefficient (β), and an estimate of the market's general return (K_m) to estimate a company's cost of retained earnings (K_s).

$$K_s = K_{rf} + \beta(K_m - K_{rf})$$

Cynical Coffee Company has a beta of 1.6. Kinda risky, but not too bad. (See the earlier section on beta for a full description of this concept!) The risk-free rate is 6%. The general rate of return on the market is 10%. So let's stick those in the CAPM formula.

$$\begin{aligned} K_s &= 6 + 1.6\,(10 - 6) \\ &= 6 + 1.6\,(4) \\ &= 12.4 \end{aligned}$$

K_s equals 6, the risk-free rate, plus 1.6, CCC's beta, times the quantity of 10, the market return, minus 6, the risk-free rate. Cynical Coffee Company's cost of retained earnings using the CAPM method is 12.4%.

Because it is difficult to determine a company's beta coefficient and there is dispute over which market should be used when estimating the market's return, many financial analysts use the bond-yield-plus-risk-premium approach instead of CAPM.

Bond-Yield-Plus-Risk-Premium Approach

The logic behind the simplistic **bond-yield-plus-risk-premium** approach is that businesses with high-interest rate debt will also have risky, high-cost equity. Using this logic, analysts simply take a company's interest rate on its own long-term debt (the coupon rate the company gives on its bonds with maturities over 10 years) and add three to seven percentage points to adjust for risk.

$$K_s = i + (3 - 7)$$

For example, a solid company like IBM might have bonds that yield 7%. So, you could estimate its cost of equity as 7% plus a 3% risk premium and get 10% for an estimated cost of retained earnings. On the other hand, a riskier company like Cynical Coffee Company may have a bond that yields 9%. When you add a 4% risk premium to that, you get 13% for an estimated cost of equity.

Discounted Cash Flow Approach

The third method used to calculate a company's cost of retained earnings is the **discounted cash flow approach (DCF)**. The DCF is based on the principle that if a stock is growing steadily, the required rate of return will equal the company's dividend yield plus the growth rate. (Because the growth rate is difficult to determine, it will probably be provided for you.)

$$K_s = \frac{DIV_1}{Price} + g$$

Suppose CCC's stocks are selling at $54, and its next dividend will be $1.75. We know that the growth rate is 9.5%, so all we have to do is plug in the numbers and go to town.

$$K_s = \frac{1.75}{54} + (0.095)$$

$$= 0.1274$$

The cost of retained earnings, K_s, equals the dividend, 1.74 divided by the selling price, $54, plus the growth rate, 0.095. The answer is 0.1274, so we can say the cost of retained earnings, according to the discounted cash flow approach, is 12.74%.

SUMMARY

- CAPM uses the stock's risk relative to the market, or beta, to determine the cost of retained earnings.
- The bond-yield-plus-risk-premium approach uses a risk premium percentage added to the company's bond interest rate.
- The discounted cash flow approach (DCA) figures out the cost of retained earnings by adding the company's growth rate to their dividend yield.
- Of these methods, no single one is best to use at any time; the best thing to do is pick the one that seems the best based on the accuracy of your information.

0:27:40

Section E: Cost of Issuing New Common Stock

The final component of the WACC formula is the **cost of issuing new common stock**. The cost of issuing new stock is essentially the cost of retained earnings plus **flotation costs**, which are the expenses incurred through the issue of new stock.

Therefore, the cost of issuing new common stock (K_e) is equal to the expected dividend (DIV) divided by the stock price times the percentage flotation cost (1 − F), plus growth (g).

$$K_e = \frac{\text{DIV}}{\text{Price}(1 - F)} + g$$

Cynical Coffee Company issues new common stock. The price per share is $54, and the projected dividend is $1.75. We already know CCC's growth rate is 9.5%, from when we figured the discounted cash flow. For every share CCC issues, it incurs a flotation cost of $3.50. However, the flotation cost you need to use in the equation is F, which is actually the percentage of the stock price that the flotation costs represent. Just to be confusing, F is called the flotation cost.

$$F = \frac{3.5}{54} = 0.0648$$

That makes the flotation cost 3.50 divided by 54, or 0.0648.

$$\begin{aligned} K_s &= \frac{1.75}{54}(1 - 0.0648) + 0.095 \\ &= \frac{1.75}{54}(0.9352) + 0.095 \\ &= \frac{1.75}{50.50} + 0.095 \\ &= 0.034653 + 0.095 \\ &= .12965 \end{aligned}$$

So the equation is 1.75 (the dividend) divided by 54 (the price), times the quantity of 1 minus 0.0648 (the flotation cost) all plus 0.095 (the expected growth rate). With some math, the cost of common stock equals 12.97%.

Section F: Calculating the Weighted Average Cost of Capital

0:30:56

Once the cost of debt, cost of preferred stock, cost of retained earnings, and cost of issuing new common stock have been estimated, they can be combined with the company's established capital structure to calculate the overall WACC. Just plug the numbers into the WACC formula and compute.

$$\mathbf{WACC = W_d K_d(1 - T) + W_{ps} K_{ps} + W_s K_s}$$

So, let's say that Cynical Coffee Company has a target capital structure calling for 40% debt, 5% preferred stock, and 55% common equity, which is retained earnings plus common stock. Its after-tax cost of debt is 6.3%, its cost of preferred stock is 10.30%, and its cost of retained earnings using the discounted cash flow model is 12.74%.

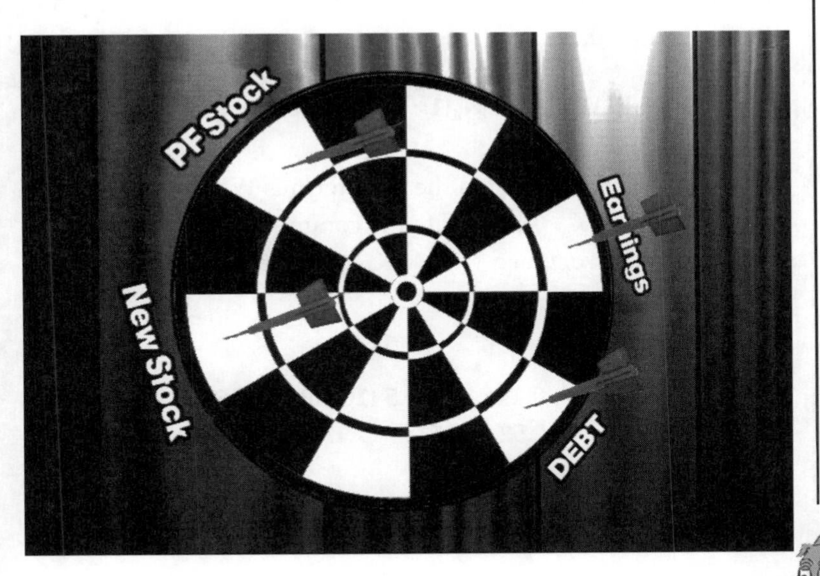

$$\text{WACC} = 0.4\ (6.3) + 0.05\ (10.30) + 0.55\ (12.74)$$
$$= 2.52\ 10.515 + 7.007$$
$$= 10.04\%$$

We take the weight of the debt, 0.4, times the cost of debt, 6.3, plus the weight of preferred stock, 0.05, times the cost of preferred stock, 10.30, plus the weight of the common equity, 0.55, times the cost of retained earnings, 12.74. We'll multiply what needs to be multiplied first, then add. That should give us an answer of 10.04%. This is the Cynical Coffee Company's weighted average cost of capital, if CCC is using retained earnings.

Note: This WACC formula assumes that the company in question has a balance in retained earnings. If the company depletes its retained earnings, it will need to issue new common stock, in which case the cost of issuing common stock would be used instead of the cost of retained earnings. In this form, the equation looks like this:

$$\text{WACC} = W_d K_d (1 - T) + W_{ps} K_{ps} + W_s K_e$$

You'll notice in this version the final term is W_s, the weight of the stock, times K_e, the cost of new common stock. This is different from above, when we use K_s, the cost of retained earnings.

$$\text{WACC} = 0.4\ (6.3) + 0.5\ (10.30) + 0.55\ (12.97)$$
$$= 2.52 + 0.515 + 7.1335$$
$$= 10.17$$

If Cynical Coffee Company runs out of retained earnings, it will need to issue new common stock. This time, we have the weight of the debt, 0.4, times the cost of debt, 6.3, plus the weight of the preferred stock, 0.05, times the cost of the preferred stock, 10.30, plus the weight of the new common stock, 0.55, times the cost of the new common stock, 12.97. After some multiplication and a little addition, we get Cynical Coffee Company's WACC when issuing new common stock: 10.17%.

0:36:10

Section G: The Marginal Cost of Capital

The **marginal cost of capital** is the cost of obtaining one more dollar of new capital.

Say Cynical Coffee Company decides to hire more coffee jerks. It cost CCC only $40 for each of the three jerks it has now. But if CCC is going to hire 28 jerks, the cost of finding them increases, because it has been found that coffee jerks do not tend to congregate in the same place. CCC will have to send people out to Boise and Edmonton, and now it's paying the equivalent of $50 for each jerk it hires. At some point along the way, the cost of hiring jerks jumped way up.

The same thing happens when you're acquiring capital. The marginal cost of capital is how much more it will cost you to get more capital than you already have. Financial people say it's how much it costs you to get one more dollar. Pretty much the same thing.

I want my two dollars! — The paperboy, Better Off Dead

SUMMARY

- The cost of capital is a percentage that represents the money you're gonna spend in the process of raising capital.
- Stocks, bonds, preferred stocks, and retained earnings are capital components; you need to figure out the cost of capital for each component before averaging them to get the weighted average cost of capital.
- The marginal cost of capital refers to the condition that occurs when the cost of capital goes up because you need to get more capital than you already have access to.
- Financial people say the marginal cost of capital is the cost of raising one new dollar of capital.

STUDY SIDEKICK

Quiz 6

1. Businesses use stocks, bonds, preferred stocks, and retained earnings to _______________________________.

2. If we say that a company is issuing debt, it is the same as saying that they are issuing _________________.

3. The _________________________ is the percentage of every dollar you raise that goes back to pay for the costs of raising that dollar.

4. The method that a company uses to organize capital components to raise capital is called its

   _______________________________.

5. The cost of capital for using specific proportions of the capital components together is called the

   ____________________________________, abbreviated as_________.

6. The ___________________________ is the market interest rate of debt minus the tax savings that result because interest is deductible.

QUIZ

7. The formula used to calculate the cost of debt is

______________________________.

8. The ______________________________ is abbreviated K_{ps}.

9. The cost of ____________________________ is equal to the rate of return required by the company's stockholders.

10. The three methods that can be used to determine the cost of retained earnings are ____________________________,

______________________________, and

______________________________.

11. The CAPM formula, which is used to estimate the cost of retained earnings, is

____.

12. When using the bond-yield-plus-risk-premium approach for estimating the cost of retained earnings, you take the company's interest rate on its own long-term debt and add

___________________ to ______________________________.

13. Equity is the combination of _______________ and

___________________.

STUDY SIDEKICK

14. The ________________________ approach, abbreviated as ________, is based on the principle that if a stock is growing at a steady rate, the required rate of return will equal the company's bond yield plus a growth rate.

15. The DCF formula for estimating the cost of retained earnings is ______________________________________.

16. __________________________ are the expenses, such as printing, that a business incurs when it issues new common stock.

17. The formula used to calculate the cost of issuing new stock is ____________________________________.

18. To determine the flotation cost (F) to be used in the above-mentioned formula, you take the cost per share and ______________ it by the _________________.

19. The WACC formula, when using retained earnings, is ____.

20 The K_s in the weighted average cost of capital formula represents the ________________________________.

QUIZ

21. If a company has depleted its retained earnings and plans to issue new common stock to raise capital, the K_s at the end of the WACC formula must be changed to

_________________________________.

22. The _____________________________ is the cost of obtaining one more dollar of new capital than you already have.

23. Every company has a _____________________________ that defines the ideal percentage of debt, preferred stock, common stock, and retained earnings that it will use to raise capital.

24. Managing the company's capital structure is one of the responsibilities of the _____________________________.

25. When a company determines that it needs to raise more capital than it already has, its cost of capital

______________________.

Soon the workbook will turn against you because it's lonely. Go buy another workbook to keep this one company.

0:38:38

The Basics of Capital Budgeting

0:38:45

Section A: What Is Capital Budgeting?

Capital budgeting is the process of analyzing investment prospects and making long-term investment decisions based on that analysis. **Capital investments** (such as the acquisition of another business or investment in new equipment) require large amounts of capital and last for many years. They can dramatically affect the direction and success of a business.

Capital investments are often responsible for the success or failure of a business. Capital budgeting is a crucial aspect of a business's financial management, because it is the process used to determine which capital investments to undertake.

Although upper-level financial managers often make capital budgeting decisions, any staff member of a business can generate the ideas for capital budgeting projects. Capital investment ideas may be proposed by:

$ A company's line workers.

$ Midlevel managers.

$ Upper level managers.

However, the reality of business is that often, the same upper-level managers that are responsible for the capital budgeting process often generate ideas for capital investments.

Section B: Different Kinds of Projects

0:41:14

There are three different types of capital projects (or capital investments) that a company may consider: **mandatory projects**, expansion projects, and **replacement projects**.

Mandatory Projects:

- $ Are usually required by some other entity, such as the government or a union.
- $ Are often referred to as "safety projects" because they typically relate to safety issues.
- $ Are the least frequent capital projects that businesses undertake.

Expansion Projects:

$ Are undertaken to move the business into a new market

or

$ Expand presence in an existing market.

Replacement projects replace old, damaged, or obsolete equipment.

Section C: Isn't This Capital Budgeting Stuff Similar to Stock Valuation?

0:43:34

Analyzing potential capital projects is similar to the process used to analyze and value securities. Once a capital investment idea is generated and is determined to be worth further analysis, the financial manager begins to evaluate the project's potential value to the business.

I think I'd eat dog. I mean, I didn't decide it was okay to eat cow. Who am I to say it's not okay to eat dog?
— Eric the Barbarian

The financial manager is concerned with the same issues as a private securities investor:

> **Is the proposed project worth the costs that will be incurred to undertake it?**

Determining the value of a potential capital budgeting project is difficult. However, there are six basic steps in the evaluation process:

1. Determine the cost of the project.
2. Estimate the expected cash flows that the project will create.
3. Estimate the riskiness of the projected cash flows.
4. Determine the cost of capital at which the cash flows should be discounted.

5. Estimate the revenues of the project by using the expected cash flows to calculate a present value.

6. Compare the present value of the expected cash flows to the required outlay. If the PV of the cash flows is greater than the cost, accept the project. If the PV of the cash flows is less than the cost, reject the project. Bingo!

0:46:06

Section D: Capital Budgeting Decision Methods

The six basic methods used to decide whether to accept a particular capital project are **payback, discounted payback, net present value, profitability index, internal rate of return,** and **modified internal rate of return.**

Payback

The **payback method** calculates the number of years for a capital project to "break even," or for the revenue the project generates to equal the project's cost. Most businesses establish a maximum payback period acceptable for new capital investments. Therefore, if a potential project's payback period exceeds the company's maximum, it will be rejected. Furthermore, if a business is deciding between several capital projects, it will often choose to accept the project with the shortest payback period.

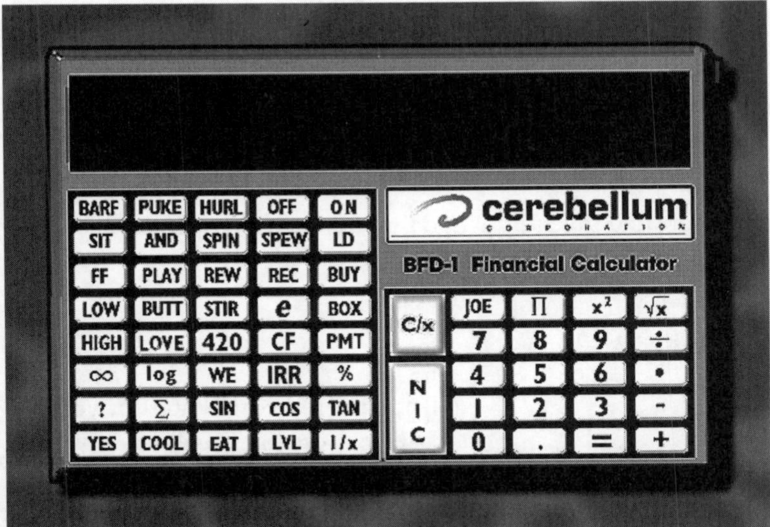

STUDY SIDEKICK

Calculating a project's payback period is rather simple with the use of a calculator. First, the expected cash flows must be entered into the calculator to determine the year in which the project breaks even. Then, the exact payback period is determined using the payback formula.

Let's say that United Prickly Pear Corporation (UPPC) is evaluating whether to purchase equipment to can prickly pears. For the sake of our example, the project would result in the following cash flows:

Year 0: −1,200

Year 1: 600

Year 2: 500

Year 3: 400

Year 4: 200

Using a calculator, we enter the cash flow of year 0 as −1,200 (negative because it's money we paid out) and add each successive year's cash flow until the calculator returns a positive answer. In our example, the third cash flow makes our answer positive, so payback occurred sometime during year 3.

To determine precisely when the project will reach payback, use the following formula:

Payback =

$$\text{Year before payback} + \frac{\text{Unrecovered cost at start of year}}{\text{Cashflow during break–even year}}$$

In our example, that's 2 (the year before payback) plus $100 (the amount of cash we needed before year 3 was added) divided by 400 (the cash flow of year 3).

$$\textbf{Payback} = 2 + \frac{100}{400}$$

$$= 2.25$$

After a little bit of quick math, we see that payback occurred after 2.25 years.

Discounted Payback

The **discounted payback method** is similar to the payback method. However, the discounted payback method adjusts the project's revenues by the cost of capital. Because the discounted payback method accounts for the time value of money, it is considered a more accurate method for determining a project's payback period.

To calculate a project's discounted payback period:

Discount all of the appropriate cash flows by dividing them by the quantity of one plus the cost of capital raised to the power of their period (or year).

Discounted payback =

$$CF_0 + \frac{CF_1}{(1+k)} + \frac{CF_2}{(1+k)^2} + \frac{CF_3}{(1+k)^3}$$

Incidentally, this is exactly the same as multiplying each cash flow by the PVIF of the cost of capital and the year of the cash flow. You can do it either way.

Once you have all those present values, the procedure is exactly the same as normal payback. In the video, we set up a little chart to make things easier. You certainly don't have to do that every time, though.

	CF	Discounted CF	Cumulative CF
Year 0	**−1200**	**−1200**	**−1200**
Year 1	**600**	**545.45**	**−654.55**
Year 2	**500**	**413.22**	**−241.33**
Year 3	**400**	**300.53**	**59.2**
Year 4	**200**	**136.60**	**not necessary**

This chart summarizes all the stages of calculating a DCF. In the first column are your cash flows. The second column shows the present values of those cash flows (you found that by dividing the cash flow by the appropriate PVIF). The third column, Cumulative CF, is a summary of what your calculator reads as you enter the cash flows.

So you can see, again, payback was sometime in year 3. Now let's figure out *when* during year 3 payback occurs.

$$\textbf{Payback} =$$

$$\textbf{Year before payback} + \frac{\textbf{Unrecovered cost at start of year}}{\textbf{Cash flow during breakeven year}}$$

$$\textbf{Payback} = 2 + \frac{241.33}{300.53}$$

$$\textbf{Payback} = 2.8 \textbf{ years}$$

See? it's the same way we figured out normal payback. Though the discounted payback method does improve the payback method by accounting for the time value of money, neither payback method accounts for the cash flows that occur following the payback period.

Net Present Value

The third method used in the capital budgeting process is **net present value**, abbreviated **NPV**. This method is essentially an accounting of a capital project's benefits versus its costs. It accounts for the time value of money and the cash flows that occur throughout the entire economic life of the asset.

Employing the NPV method, you discount the project's revenues using the present value formula, then add all the revenues together and finally subtract the project's investment to determine whether the project makes money for the business. If the net present value of a potential project is positive, the business will make money and the project is accepted. If a project's NPV is negative, it will be rejected, because the NPV suggests the company will lose money.

VIDEO NOTES

The three steps to the NPV method:

1. **Calculate the present value of each cash flow.**
2. **Add all the present values.**
3. **Subtract the project's initial investment outlay to get the NPV.**

Let's say Strongarm Willy's Strikebreaking Service wants to move into a new field: rental of all-purpose goons. Strongarm Willy's believes it will need to spend $10,000 on equipment for the project—you know, clubs, ice picks, other weapons. The $10,000 in equipment is the new asset that Willy will have to decide whether to invest in.

The accountants project $7,000 revenue for the first year, $3,500 for the second, $1,500 for the third, and $1,000 for the fourth. After four years, Willy will evaluate the program and decide whether to buy more equipment.

The NPV formula is the cash flow of year 1, CF_1, divided by the quantity of one plus the cost of capital raised to the first power, plus the cash flow of year 2, CF_2, divided by the quantity of one plus the cost of capital raised to the second power, and so on. Since Strongarm Willy's is only marginally legal, it's fairly expensive for it to raise capital. The cost of capital is 20%.

$$\frac{\mathbf{7{,}000}}{\mathbf{(1 + 0.2)^1}} + \frac{\mathbf{3{,}500}}{\mathbf{(1 + 0.2)^2}} + \frac{\mathbf{1{,}500}}{\mathbf{(1 + 0.2)^3}} + \frac{\mathbf{1{,}000}}{\mathbf{(1 + 0.2)^4}} =$$

STUDY SIDEKICK

Divide 7,000 by 1 + 0.2, the cost of capital, and raise that to the first power, because it's the first period of time. Add 3,500 divided by (1 + 0.2) to the second power, and so on.

$$\frac{7,000}{1.2} + \frac{3,500}{1.44} + \frac{1,500}{1.728} + \frac{1,000}{2.0736} =$$

Simplify a little. Now we have 7,000 over 1.2, plus 3,500 over 1.44, plus 1,500 over 1.728, plus 1,000 over 2.0736.

$$5833.33 + 2430.55 + 868.06 + 482.25 = 9614.19$$

Divide those, and we get 5,833.33 plus 2,430.55 plus 868.06, plus 482.25, which equals $9,614.19.

The total discounted cash flow is $9,614.19. Since that's the discounted cash flow, that's how much Strongarm Willy's expects to make in today's dollars.

Now, let's subtract the initial investment, $10,000, to get the net present value. Remember, the net present value is the present value of the cash flows minus the investment.

$$9,614.19 - 10,000 = -385.81$$

If we subtract the $10,000 investment from the present value of the cash flows, $9,614.19, we get negative 385.81.

The negative NPV suggests we should reject this plan.

Though the net present value does account for the time value of money and future cash flows, using this method to compare two projects is very difficult.

Profitability Index

The fourth method used in the capital budgeting process uses many of the same concepts as the NPV method. However, the primary use of the **profitability index**, or **PI**, is to compare projects of different sizes. The PI does so by comparing the present values of the cash flows.

The profitability index uses the NPV of a project's cash flows as well as the initial investment to calculate the value of the project per dollar spent. To calculate the PI of a capital project, simply divide the present value of the cash inflows by the value of the investment.

$$\mathbf{PI} = \frac{\textbf{PV of cash inflows}}{\textbf{investment}}$$

If a business were evaluating two different projects both with positive NPVs, the business could use the PI calculation to determine which project would offer a better return per dollar that it invests.

Let's say Strongarm Willy's has two different projects it might invest in. The first project, project A, requires spending $1 million to set up a network of safe houses around the country. The other project, project B, costs $100,000 to get new bludgeons for all of Strongarm Willy's goons. Project A returns an NPV of $50,000, and project B returns an NPV of $40,000.

Calculating the PI is pretty easy: Just divide the present value of the cash inflows by the value of the investment. So in our example with Strongarm Willy's, the PI of project A equals 1,050,000 divided by 1,000,000, or 1.05. The PI of project B is 140,000 divided by 100,000, or 1.40.

Project A: $\frac{1{,}050{,}000}{1{,}000{,}000} = 1.05$

Project B: $\frac{140{,}000}{100{,}000} = 1.40$

These numbers show what Willy gets back for each dollar he invests. With project A, Willy gets back a dollar and five cents for every dollar he invests. Project B's return of a dollar and forty cents per dollar is much better. If Willy doesn't have enough money to spend on both projects, the profitability index can be pretty helpful.

Internal Rate of Return

I'm connected to you by more than just sturdy twine. — Brian Coleman

The fifth decision method used in the capital budgeting process is the **internal rate of return**, abbreviated **IRR**. The internal rate of return is the discount rate that forces the present value of the project's expected cash inflows to equal the present value of the project's expected costs. The only way to calculate the IRR without a calculator is through trial and error, which can be rather tedious. However, calculating the IRR of a particular project is rather simple when you use a financial calculator.

To calculate a capital project's IRR using a financial calculator:

1. **Enter all of the cash flows into the calculator's cash flow register (including the initial investment, which is the cash flow for time period 0).**
2. **Press the IRR button.**

Strongarm Willy's cash flows with the calculator:

CF 0: $−10,000

CF 1: $7,000

CF 2: $3,500

CF 3: $1,500

CF 4: $1,000

IRR = 17.07

We'll use Strongarm Willy's cash flows again. Enter negative 10,000 for the initial investment, then press CFi or CF0, depending on your calculator. Now we input the rest of the cash flows: 7,000 for year 1, 3,500 for year 2, 1,500 for year 3, 1,000 for year 4. Now tell the calculator to compute by pressing IRR. The answer: 17.07! That means the internal rate of return is 17.07%.

Once the IRR has been calculated, it can be compared with the project's cost of capital. If a project's IRR is equal to or greater than its cost of capital, the project will return more than it

cost to raise the money for the initial investment. If a project's IRR is less than its cost of capital, undertaking the project will lose money for the business.

The IRR is the capital budgeting decision method that business executives prefer. Although academics agree that the NPV method is more accurate, business executives favor the IRR because they prefer to analyze investments based on rates of return as opposed to present value dollars, and the IRR method is more conducive to comparing different projects.

However, **the IRR is less than perfect**. The IRR method assumes that a project's revenues are being reinvested into the same project. Unfortunately, businesses do not often have the luxury of investing all revenues directly back into a project.

Modified Internal Rate of Return

V3

VIDEO NOTES

Modified Internal Rate of Return

The sixth and final decision-making method used in the capital budgeting process does not make the same assumptions as the IRR method. The **modified internal rate of return (MIRR)** is the discount rate that forces the present value of the project's cost to equal the present value of its terminal value. In using terminal value, the MIRR method assumes that the company will reinvest a project's revenues into the company but not necessarily into the same project. The terminal value is the sum of future values of a project's cash inflows.

To calculate a capital project's modified internal rate of return:

1. **Determine the project's terminal value by multiplying each cash flow by 1 plus the cost of capital raised to the number of years it is compounded. Then add the future values to get the terminal value.**
2. **Enter the numbers into a financial calculator. First, enter the investment (a negative number representing year 0). Then enter 0 for the subsequent cash flows. Then, enter the terminal value for the last period.**
3. **Press the IRR button to get the MIRR.**

Let's use the cash flows from Strongarm Willy's. Using this little timetable, we'll figure out the terminal value. We're figuring out the future value for each cash flow, the long way. That means we're going to multiply each cash flow by 1 plus the cost of capital, raised to the number of years it's compounded.

Study Sidekick

There's no future value for the *investment*, because that's a cash outflow. We're assuming, by the way, that Strongarm Willy's cost of capital is 14%.

Year 0	Year 1	Year 2	Year 3	Year 4
−10,000	7,000	3,500	1,500	1,000
	$(1.14)^3$	$(1.14)^2$	$(1.14)^1$	nc
	10,370.81	4,548.60	1,710	1,000

Year 1: 7,000 times 1.14 raised to the third power, which is 10,370.81.

Year 2: 3,500 times 1.14 raised to the second power. That's 4,548.60.

Year 3: 1,500 times 1.14 raised to the first power. That's 1,710.

Year 4: Doesn't get compounded, so that's just 1,000.

10,370 + 4,548.60 + 1,710 + 1,000 = 17,629.41

Now we'll add those future values to get the terminal value. The terminal value is $17,629.41.

Now enter the numbers into the calculator. Year 0 is −10,000 for the dough we shelled out to start the project. Enter 0 for years 1 through 3. The calculator doesn't know how many periods there are unless you enter those zeros. Then enter the terminal value for year 4.

The sequence ends up being like this.

CF_0	**+/−10000**
CF_1	**0**
CF_2	**0**
CF_3	**0**
CF_4	**17629.41**
IRR	

That returns an MIRR of 15.23%. We compare this with Strongarm Willy's cost of capital, which is 14%. The MIRR is greater than the cost of capital, which would suggest that Strongarm Willy's should undertake the project.

"About 43% of Americans, for example, doubted that humans are descended from other animal species and about 45% said that early humans lived at the same time as the dinosaurs."

National Science Board

QUIZ

Quiz 7

1. ______________________ is an important application of financial concepts. It is the process of analyzing investment prospects and making long-term decisions based on that analysis.

2. ______________ investments are enormous in scope and can make or break a business.

3. The acquisition of another business, investment in new equipment, and new product development are all examples of ______________________________.

4. Although they can come from anywhere, most capital budgeting projects are developed by ____________________________ of a business.

5. The three basic kinds of capital projects are ______________________, ________________________, and ________________________.

6. ______________________, or safety projects, are those that some other entity, such as the government, requires.

7. ______________________ are projects in which old, damaged, or obsolete equipment is replaced.

8. ___________________________ are investments made to move into a new market or expand within an existing market.

9. The six basic steps for evaluating the financial viability of a potential capital budgeting project are

   1. ____
      ____
   2. ____
      ____
   3. ____
      ____
   4. ____
      ____
   5. ____
      ____
   6. ____

10. If the present value of the cash flows of a potential capital budgeting project is less than the required outlay for the project, the company should _________________ the project.

QUIZ

11. The six basic methods that can be used to decide whether to accept a project are ____________________, ____________________, ____________________, ____________________, ____________________, and ____________________.

12. The ______________ method calculates the number of years required for a project to break even.

13. A ____________ payback period is better than a ____________ payback period. Therefore, if a business is deciding between two projects, it will usually pick the one with the ____________ payback period.

14. The formula used to calculate the payback period of a project is ______________________________.

15. The first step in using the discounted payback method is to discount all the appropriate cash flows. The formula used to do this is ______________________________.

16. The two main limitations to using the payback method are ______________________________ and ______________________________.

Study Sidekick

17. The discounted payback method does account for the time value of money, but still ignores ______________________.

18. The ____________________________ method discounts a project's revenues using the present value formula and then adds all the revenues to the project's investment to determine whether the project makes or loses money.

19. The three steps to analyzing a capital project using the net present value method are ________________________, ______________________, and ______________________.

20. If the NPV of a project is ________________, the business should reject the project.

21. The primary use of the ______________________ is to compare projects of different sizes using the present values of the cash flows.

22. The formula used to calculate the PI is ______________________________.

23. The internal rate of return is the discount rate that forces the ____ to equal the ____________________________________.

Quiz

24. Once you have calculated a project's IRR, you compare it with the business' ________________________. If the IRR is greater than the ____________________, the project will return __________ money than it cost to raise the money for the project.

25. Most business executives prefer the _______ ______________ method for capital budgeting.

26. The ______________________________ is the discount rate that forces the present value of the project's cost to equal the present value of its terminal value.

27. Terminal value is the

____.

28. If the MIRR is _______________ than the cost of capital, the company should undertake the project.

29. If you are a martyr, you can calculate IRR through trial and error, or you can use a ______________________ and make your life much easier.

30. The IRR method assumes that the revenues from a project are being ________________________, which sometimes a company cannot do.

1:14:14

Capital Budgeting With Certainty

1:14:20

Section A: What are We Doing?

An important step in the capital budgeting process is the estimation of a business's cash flows.

A **cash flow** is an accounting of the actual hard cash that comes in and out of a business. Cash flows that directly relate to a particular project are **incremental cash flows** because they reflect the difference that the project makes on operations.

Section B: The Cash Flows and the Process

A company that is evaluating a capital investment will generate three different types of cash flows: the net investment cash outlay (NICO), operating cash flows (OCFs), and the **net disposal cash flow**.

The **net investment cash outlay,** or **NICO**, is all of the money required to initiate a particular capital project. The NICO typically includes any new equipment that must be purchased for the capital project, plus the corresponding transportation and modification costs, charges to the company's net working capital for inventory, and so on.

Study Sidekick

Operating Cash Flows, or **OCFs**, represent the change in a company's cash flows directly resulting from a capital project, or the actual cash that the company is receiving because of the project. OCFs are calculated annually over the life of the capital project.

To calculate the OCFs for a capital project, simply subtract the operating and depreciation costs from the total revenues of the project to get the taxable income for the project. Then, subtract income taxes to get the net income (the taxes need to be subtracted because we are interested in calculating the after-tax weighted average cost of capital). Finally, add back the depreciation costs (because depreciation costs are not actual cash outflow).

OCF = revenue − operating expenses − depreciation − taxes + depreciation

The net disposal cash flow is the final cash flow resulting from the termination of a capital project. It is a cash inflow for the business because the business will make money through liquidation of the project's remaining assets.

STANDARD DEVIANT FINANCIAL INFO:

The net disposal cash flow isn't always an inflow. Sometimes the cost of cleaning up after your asset is more than the proceeds for selling it. In that case, the net disposal cash flow would be a cash outflow.

Two steps are required to calculate the net disposal cash flow for a particular capital project:

1. Estimate the cash that will be received from the liquidation process, subtract any **removal costs**, and then subtract the applicable taxes.
2. Determine the change in net working capital that will occur because the capital project has terminated.

Net disposal cash flow = liquidation cash − removal costs − taxes + net working capital

Captain Blahr's Cash Flows

So let's take a look at the NICO for Captain Blahr's company.

NICO

Ship (equipment)	$ 8,000.00
Increase in NWC	$ 3,000.00
Cash outflow	$ 11,000.00

As we can see, the NICO includes two parts. The equipment is the cost of the ship and the cost of transporting it, which totals $8,000. Also included in the NICO are the increases to net working capital, which are $3,000. Added together, these two costs equal the cash outflow or NICO, of $11,000.

This takes us to the next step, which is calculating the yearly cash flows. Let's look at what we have. Examine figure A.

"There are two sorts of truth: trivialities, where opposites are obviously absurd, and profound truths, recognized by the fact that the opposite is also a profound truth."

Niels Bohr

Figure A: Scourge II Cash Flow Sheet

NICO

Ship (equipment)	8,000.00
Increase in NWC	3,000.00
Cash outflow	10,000.00

Cash inflows

	Years			
	0	1	2	3
Revenue		9,000.00	9,000.00	9,000.00
Expenses		5,000.00	5,000.00	5,000.00
NOI		4,000.00	4,000.00	4,000.00
Depreciation		2,460.00	3,600.00	1,200.00
EBT		1,360.00	400.00	2,800.00
Taxes (30%)		408.00	120.00	840.00
NI		952.00	280.00	1,960.00
Add back Depreciation		2,640.00	3,600.00	1,960.00
OCF		3,592.00	3,880.00	3,160.00
Sale price + NWC				3,500.00
Actual Cash Flows:	<11,000.00>	3,592.00	3,880.00	6,660.00
Present value @ 14%		3,151.00	2,986.00	4,496.00

You can see that for years 1 through 3 we have the revenue of $9,000, followed by the expenses, which are $5,000 a year. That leaves us with the net operating income, or NOI.

Now, we use the **modified accelerated cost recovery system**, or **MACRS**, to determine the depreciation values for Captain Blahr's ship. We'll put the table for that right here.

Scourge Depreciation Sheet

Depreciable base	**8,000**	**8,000**	**8,000**
MACRS rate	**0.33**	**0.45**	**0.15**
	2,640	**3,600**	**1,200**

The 3-year MACRS rates are 33% in year 1, 45% in year 2, and 15% in year 3. We multiply those by the value of Scourge II, and we get the depreciation values for years 1, 2, and 3. Now we can look back on figure A and see where those are filled in.

Subtracting the depreciation values, we get the next line, which is earning before taxes, or EBT. That doesn't get to stay a figure very long, because taxes are subtracted next to get the net income, or NI. Finally, we add depreciation back, and our final answers (for this stage, at least) are the operating cash flows, or OCFs.

Now comes the tricky task of determining the net disposal cash flow, which I'm sure you remember is the sale price of the asset

plus the return on the net working capital (NWC). The return on NWC is easy, but for the sale of the ship, we'll have to calculate the capital gains taxes.

Sale price	**475**
Book value	**560**
Capital gain/loss	**−85**
Taxes	**0.3**
Capital gains tax	**−25**

In actuality, the calculation of capital gains taxes isn't that difficult, either. We subtract the book value of the ship from its sale price. This gives us our capital gain, or in this case, our capital loss. Then, we multiply the capital gain or loss by the tax rate to get the tax implications of the sale, which, as we can see above, result in \$−25, or a \$25 tax credit.

Sale price	**475**
Less capital gains tax	**−25**
Plus change in NWC	**3,000**
Net disposal CF	**3,500**

So add it all together—the sale price of the ship, the tax credit, and the return on net working capital—to get the net disposal cash flow, which is \$3,500.

1:29:18

So, the net disposal cash flow is added to the year 3 OCF, to yield the final year's actual cash flow, or $6,660. You can see below that we went ahead and found the present values of the actual cash flows, using the PVIFs of 14% and the appropriate period.

Year 1: 3,592 (PVIF[14%,1])   3,592(0.8772)=3,151

Year 2: 3,880 (PVIF[14%,2])   3,880(0.7695)=2,986

Year 3: 6,660 (PVIF[14%,3])   6,660(0.6750)=4,496

Section C: Evaluation of a Capital Budget

Now we're going to run through the calculations for all six of the decision methods for capital budgeting.

Payback

We start with the investment or NICO:	− 11,000
Then add year 1 cash flow.	+ 3,592
The calculator returns:	− 7,408
Keep going. Add year 2.	+ 3,880
The calculator says:	− 3,528
Keep going. Add year 3.	+ 6,660
The calculator returns:	3,132

BINGO!

That means payback was in year 2. To figure out exactly when, we divide year 2's unrecovered cash by year 3's cash flow, and then add 2 because payback occurred that year.

$$\frac{3{,}528}{6{,}660} + 2 = 2.53$$

3,528 divided by 6,660 plus 2 equals a payback of 2.53 years.

Discounted Payback

The next method is discounted payback. This is the same as payback, but instead of the final cash flows, we'll use the present values of the cash flows.

Start with year 0 cash outlay:	−11,000
Add year 1.	+ 3,151
The calculator says:	−7,849
Add year 2.	+ 2,986
And the calculator returns:	−4,863
Keep going. Add year 3.	+ 4,496
Now the calculator says:	−367

Hey! Still negative! That means it's impossible to figure a discounted payback for this project—it will never pay back what we spent on it. That's bad.

Net Present Value

The third capital budgeting decision method is the net present value method. For this, we just add together all the present values and the investment.

Investment	**−11,000**
Year 1	**3,151**
Year 2	**2,986**
Year 3	**+ 4,496**
Total	**−367**

The negative NPV means if we undertake this project we'll lose money.

REJECT!

STUDY SIDEKICK

Profitability Index

We divide the present value of the benefits (those would be the present values of the cash inflows) by the value of the investments—that's the $11,000 we spent to set everything up.

$$3{,}151 + 2{,}986 + 4{,}496 = 10{,}633$$

$$\frac{10{,}633}{11{,}000} = 0.967$$

The present value of benefits for years 1 through 3 is 3,151 plus 2,986 plus 4,496, which equals 10,633. Divide 10,633 by the present value of the costs, 11,000, and you get a profitability index of 0.967. That's less than a dollar return for every dollar spent. Yuck!

Internal Rate of Return

We just put all the cash flows into the calculator and press IRR.

	−11,000	**for CF_0**
Now enter	**3,592**	**for CF_1**
And then	**3,880**	**for CF_2**
And then	**6,660**	**for CF_3**

Now press IRR.

The calculator says 12.19%.

This answer is less than the cost of capital, so we're wasting money.

Boo.

Modified Internal Rate of Return

First we find the terminal value by adding the future values of all the cash flows.

Year 1

$$3{,}880\ (1 + K)^n = 3{,}880\ (1.14)^2 = 4{,}668$$

Multiply 3,592 times 1 plus the cost of capital, or 1.14. Raise that to the number of compounding periods. There are two compounding periods, so we'll raise it to the second power.

Year 2

$$3{,}880\ (1 + K)^n = 3{,}880\ (1.14)^1 =$$

Multiply 3,568 times 1.14 raised to the first power because it gets compounded once.

Year 3

Year 3 doesn't get a chance to get compounded because it's the last year.

ADD THE FUTURE VALUES!

$$4{,}668 + 4{,}423 + 7{,}116 = 15{,}751$$

15,751 is the terminal value.

STUDY SIDEKICK

1:35:10

Now we enter the investment (negative 11,000) into the calculator, along with the terminal value. Remember to put as many cash flows with 0 in between them as you have other periods. For us, there will be two zeros. Here's the actual keystroke procedure:

11,000	
+/–	$\mathbf{CF_i}$
0	$\mathbf{CF_i}$
0	$\mathbf{CF_i}$
15,571	$\mathbf{CF_i}$
IRR	

When we tell our machine to calculate the IRR, it says **12.71%**.

Again, less than the cost of capital. This project sucks.

Section D: Capital Budgeting for Replacement

Here's our second and final example in capital budgeting: capital budgeting for replacement.

By the way, while we're thinking about it, this example is the best example of incremental cash flows. By what increment is this new asset going to improve things? The whole point of capital budgeting for replacement is to see if the new thing is better than the old. The difference between the old cash flow and the new cash flow is the increment.

"Marvelous what ideas young people have these days. But I don't believe a word of it."

Einstein

In this example, we'll explore what happens when Z-Co bed company purchases a new piece of equipment, a trimmer, to replace the old trimmer.

STUDY SIDEKICK

The old trimmer cost $3,250, and is being depreciated on a straight line basis over ten years, making the depreciation $325 each year. The old trimmer has been in service for five years, and the managers expected that the trimmer would be worthless after ten years of use. That means five years of depreciation are left, giving the trimmer a $1,625 current book value.

The new supertrimmer is a bit more expensive—its on-board computer pushes the trimmer's cost to $10,000. The new trimmer would also involve an increase of $1,000 in net working capital. Though the new trimmer is more delicate, and has a life span of five years, the engineers say it will save the company $3,000 in expenses per year over the old trimmer.

What's even better is that in five years we will be able to sell the trimmer for $3,000. The old trimmer has a market value of $500, which is a lot less than its book value. Remember, the market value is how much you can get for selling your asset to some stooge on the street. The book value is the price of the new asset minus accumulated depreciation. Z-Co, like any other good company, should have the book value laying around in its accounting records somewhere.

The other facts we need to know:

- The tax rate is 40% on revenue.
- Z-Co's cost of capital is 11%.
- The new trimmer would fall into the government's MACRS three-year depreciation class.

Look on the next page for the chart for this puppy.

Z-Co Trimmer Replacement

	Year 0	Year 1	Year 2	Year 3	Year 4	Year 5
Cost of new equipment	<10,000>					
Market value of old equipment	500					
Tax savings on sale	450					
Increase in NWC	<1,000>					
Total outlay	<10,050>					
After tax decrease in cost		1,800	1,800	1,800	1,800	1,800
Tax savings from depreciation		1,190	1,670	470	150	<130>
OCF		2,990	3,470	2,270	1,950	1,670
Net disposal CF						2,800
Net cash flow	<10,050>	2,990	3,470	2,270	1,950	4,470
PV @ 11%	<10,050>	2,693	2,816	1,659	1,285	2,652

NICO

Let's look at the NICO first. Here you see the initial cost of the new trimmer, the amount of money we get from selling the old one, and the tax implications of the sale. Since we would sell the old trimmer below the book value, we would get a tax benefit of $450. Finally, there will be an increase in net working capital of $1,000—this covers stuff like buying supplies of thread for the trimmer. The net investment for Year 0 is $10,050. Again, we'll record it as a negative because it's money we're paying out.

Cost of new equipment	**−10,000**
Market value of old equipment	**500**
Tax savings on sale	**450**
Increase in NWC	**− 1,000**
Total outlay	**−10,050**

Now where did that tax money come from? Hold on, we'll show you.

Sale price of trimmer	**500**
Subtract book value of old	**− 1,625**
Capital loss	**1,125**
Multiply by the tax rate	**0.40**
Tax savings	**450**

We subtract the book value of $1,625 from the sales price of $500 and get a capital loss of $1,125. Multiply the capital loss by the tax rate of 40% and we get the tax savings on the sale of $450.

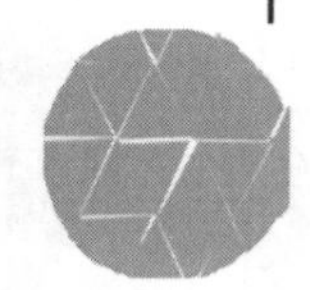

Changes to Cash Flows

Now let's figure the individual cash flows for each year we have the new trimmer. We're mainly interested in how the new trimmer changes the cash flows. We already know that it will decrease costs by $3,000 a year which, after taxes of 40%, is $1,800. The other main difference the new trimmer will create is a tax savings on depreciation.

Depreciation

Because the new machine will depreciate much faster than the old one, we'll get more of a tax break than we did before. So what we have to do is calculate how much of a benefit the new depreciation will create, then subtract the old **depreciation benefit**, so we know how much better the new is than the old.

	Year 1	Year 2	Year 3	Year 4	Year 5
Value of new machine	10,000	10,000	10,000	10,000	10,000
MARCS rates	0.33	0.45	0.15	0.07	0
Depreciation benefit	3,300	4,500	1,500	700	0
Dep. benefit of old machine	325	325	325	325	325
New depreciation benefit	2,975	4,175	1,175	375	−325
Tax rate	0.40	0.40	0.40	0.40	0.40
Tax savings from depreciation	1190	1670	470	150	−130

We have the depreciable value, which is the price of the new machine. On our chart, we have years 1 through 5, and the price of the trimmer under each. You can also see MACRS rates for those years listed under the those. With a little quick multiplication, we have the figures for the next row, which are the depreciations of the new trimmer for each year. Since the old machine was straight line depreciated for ten years, we can just

fill in its yearly depreciation value of $325. Now we can subtract the value of depreciation on the old machine from the value of the new machine's depreciation to get the savings on depreciation.

Okay, now we know how much more the new machine depreciates. That's called the depreciation benefit—because it's what we use to calculate the tax savings from depreciation. If we just multiply this by the annual tax rate of 40%, we get the tax savings on the depreciation of the new machine. These numbers are exactly how much the new machine would save us in depreciation.

We now have the net operating cash flows for each year, which are the after-tax increases in cash flow, plus the tax savings from depreciation.

Net Disposal Cash Flow

Sale price	3,000
Book value	0
Capital gain	3,000
Tax rate	0.4
Tax	1,200

Liquidation Proceeds

Sale price	3,000
Capital gains tax	−1,200
Return on NWC	1,000
Net disposal CF	2,800

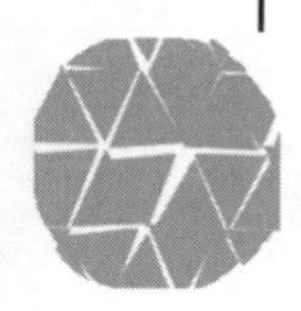

For the terminal year (you know, the last one) we need to figure out the net disposal cash flow which, compared to what we've been doing, is pretty easy. We don't even have to worry about the old machine, because we didn't keep it. It has a zero salvage value and a zero book value anyway. So, for the new trimmer, in year 5, we get a $3,000 sale price, minus the book value of 0, and multiply by 40% to get the tax liability. The book value is zero because the new trimmer will have reached its expected life span of five years. Now subtract the tax liability from the sale value, to get the trimmer's after-tax sale value of $1,800. Add the after-tax sale value of $1,800 to the return in net working capital of $1,000. We get back the $1,000 of net working capital because we assume that we can send back all that thread we were using with the new trimmer. That result is the net disposal cash flow of $2,800.

When we put that on the chart, we see that the final year cash flow is $4,470.

Finding the Present Values

Like we did the other times, we're going to figure out the present values of each of the cash flows. The PVIF we'll be using is going to be for 11% cost of capital and the appropriate number of periods.

Year 1: PV = $2,290 (PVIF[11%, 1 period])

2,693 = 2,990(0.9009)

Year 2: PV = $3,470 (PVIF[11%, 2 periods])

2,816 = 3,470(0.8116)

Year 3: PV = $2,270 (PVIF[11%, 3 periods])

1,659 = 2,270(0.7312)

Year 4: PV = $1,950 (PVIF[11%, 4 periods])

1,285 = 1,950(0.6587)

Year 5: PV = $4,470 (PVIF[11%, 5 periods])

2,652 = 4,470(0.5935)

Evaluation

Now for the decision method.

Net Present Value:

NICO	−10,050
Year 1	2,693
Year 2	2,816
Year 3	1,659
Year 4	1,285
Year 5	2,652
Net present value	1,055

The cash outflow, −10,050, plus all the cash flows' present values. That returns 1,055, which is a positive number, which is good. The positive return means Z-Co would definitely save money if and when it replaces the old trimmer. Heck, Z-Co would have enough dough to pay off its investors, and even have a little left over for fun.

Quiz 8

1. A ________________ is an accounting of the actual cash that comes in and flows out of a business.

2. Cash flows that directly relate to a particular capital project are known as ________________________________.

3. The three main types of cash flows generated by a company evaluating a capital investment are ________________________, ________________________, and ____________________________.

4. The ________________________________, abbreviated as _________, is the cash outflow that represents the money required to start a capital project.

5. ____________________________, abbreviated as __________, represent the change in a company's cash flows directly resulting from the revenues generated by a capital project. They are calculated on a(n)________________ basis throughout the life of the project.

"I am not Spock."

Leonard Nimoy

Quiz

6. The OCFs for a capital project are equal to ____________minus____________minus____________ minus______________plus______________.

7. The final cash flow resulting from the ending of a capital project is known as the ______________________________.

8. ________________ is the process of selling off the remaining assets of a capital project.

9. The costs a business incurs from the process of selling off remaining assets are known as __________________ costs.

10. Net disposal cash flow is made up of

____________________________________.

This time, we're not going to try some cheap gimmick to get you to buy more workbooks.

Buy more workbooks.

PRACTICE EXAM 2

Okay, you've gotten through the rest of the material, it's time to test yourself again. The following self-test consists of 30 multiple choice questions and 5 word problems. Take your time and work through each question. When you're finished, check your answers with the answer key—but NO CHEATING!

1. The rate of return is:

- **a.** the minimum return that an investor demands on an investment
- **b.** a percentage that leads to money that you, as an investor, don't keep
- **c.** the amount of money that an investor earns back on an investment
- **d.** the interest rate used in determining the present value of a lump sum

2. The future value of $1,000 in 4 years earning 8% annually is:

- **a.** $3,246
- **b.** $1,360
- **c.** $1,851
- **d.** $735

Test Yourself

3. The present value of a 20-year annual annuity of $500, with a 5% expected return, is:

   a. $6,231.11
   b. $10,000.00
   c. $16.533.00
   d. $6,118.26

4. The present value of $200 per year in perpetuity if the current discount rate is 7% would be:

   a. $2,857.14
   b. $1,400.00
   c. $2,864.84
   d. $4,280.00

5. If the current discount rate is 8%, the present value of a bond with a 6% coupon rate, annual coupon payments, and a $1,000 par value at a maturity in 15 years is:

   a. $858.45
   b. $1,000.00
   c. $828.77
   d. $1,171.15

6. The bond in question 5 is being sold for $900, is that a good deal?

   a. yes
   b. no

7. Assuming that five years of the bond in question 5's maturity have passed, its present value is:

   a. $877.07
   b. $999.96
   c. $1152.30
   d. $865.80

8. An outstanding bond may sell at a discount if:

   a. market interest rates have decreased
   b. the company that issued the bond is now bankrupt
   c. market interest rates have risen
   d. the time remaining until maturity has decreased

TEST YOURSELF

9. The formula used to calculate the premium that should be added to an outstanding bond with a coupon rate that is higher than market interest rates is:

a. (coupon payment on new bond – coupon payment on outstanding bond)

b. [coupon payment on new bond][PVIFA (old rate, periods til maturity)]

c. (coupon payment on outstanding bond – coupon payment on new bond) (PVIF@new rate, maturity on old bond)

d. (coupon payment on outstanding bond – coupon payment on new bond) [PVIFA i(new rate, periods til maturity)]

10. As interest rates go down, bond prices:

a. go down

b. go up

c. remain the same

11. The current yield on a bond that is selling for $875 with a current payment of $65 per period is:

a. 7.43%

b. 13.46%

c. 9.26%

d. 0.074%

12. The yield to call on a bond is:

a. the interest rate that an investor would receive until his or her bond is called

b. the interest rate that an investor would receive if the bond is held until maturity

c. the amount of interest that the company calling a bond will save by calling the bond

d. none of the above

13. The formula used to calculate the present value of a preferred stock is:

a. Dividend (PVIFA)

b. Dividend / market interest rate

c. Dividend / discount rate

d. Discount rate / dividend

14. The rate of return on a preferred stock with a $50 dividend and a current selling price of $900 is:

a. 6.5%

b. 7%

c. 4.5%

d. none of the above

Test Yourself

15. Using the Gordon growth model, the present value of a common stock whose last annual dividend was $4, is expected to grow at a rate of 10%, and has an expected rate of return of 12% is:

a. $195.00

b. $220.00

c. $200.00

d. $20.00

16. If the common stock in question 15 is trading at $210, would it be a good deal?

a. yes

b. no

c. not enough information given

17. Growth stocks are more valuable than nongrowth stocks.

a. true

b. false

18. The four major steps used to determine the value of a supernormal stock are:

1. Determine the present value of dividends.
2. Apply the constant growth formula.
3. Discount the normal value to PV using PVIF.
4. Discount the dividends from the normal period and add them to the present value of the stock during the supernormal period.

a. true

b. false

19. The after-tax cost of debt for a company that borrows debt at an interest rate of 7% and has an income tax rate of 40% is:

a. 3%

b. 2.8%

c. 4.2%

d. none of the above

TEST YOURSELF

20. The cost of preferred stock for a company whose preferred stock pays a $12 dividend per share, sells for $140 per share, and incurs underwriting charges of 5% per share is:

a. 8%

b. 11.66%

c. 8.57%

d. 9%

21. The three approaches that can be used to calculate the cost of retained earnings are:

a. CAPM, bond-yield-plus-risk-premium approach, WACC

b. CAPM, bond-yield-plus-risk-premium approach, discounted cash flow approach

c. CAPM, discounted cash flow approach, profitability index

d. none of the above

2. The cost of retained earnings, using the CAPM, for a company with a beta of 1.7, when the risk-free rate is 7%, and the general rate of return on the market is 11% is:

a. 25.7%

b. 12.4%

c. 18.9%

d. none of the above

23. Using the DCF equation, the cost of retained earnings for a company with a growth rate of 7.5%, a stock price of $47, and a forthcoming dividend of $2 is:

a. 11.75%

b. 17.62%

c. 9.5%

d. 3.19%

24. The cost of issuing new common stock for a company with a price per share of $47, a projected dividend of $2.50, a growth rate of 7.5%, and flotation costs of $2.50 per share is:

a. 12.45%

b. 13.12%

c. 11.5%

d. none of the above

25. The marginal cost of capital is:

a. the cost of raising capital with new common stock

b. the cost of capital divided by the company's growth rate

c. the cost of raising one more dollar of new capital

d. equal to the weighted average cost of capital

26. An example of a capital budgeting project is:

a. the acquisition of another business

b. investment in new equipment

c. new product development

d. a and b

e. all of the above

f. none of the above

27. The six basic methods used in capital budgeting decision making are:

a. payback, discounted payback, CAPM, NPV, profitability index, IRR

b. IRR, MIRR, discounted payback, profitability index, payback, NPV

c. payback, IRR, MIRR, DCF, NPV, profitability index

d. CAPM, MIRR, IRR, NPV, payback, discounted payback

"I am Spock."

Leonard Nimoy

28. The net present value of a capital project requiring an initial investment of $9,000 that is expected to have $5,000 in revenue the first year, $3,500 the second year, and $1,500 the third year with a cost of capital of 14% is:

a. $675.36

b. $908.41

c. −$432.85

d. −$908.41

29. If your company relied on the net present value method for capital budgeting decision making, would you vote to accept the project in question 28?

a. yes

b. no

c. not enough information

TEST YOURSELF

30.The following is a type of cash flow used in capital budgeting:

a. NICO

b. OCF

c. DCF

d. net disposal cash flow

e. a and b

f. all of the above

g. a, b, and d

h. a, b, and c

31. Determine the present value of the following company's supernormal growth stock:

Initial growth rate = 18%

Normal growth rate after two years = 8%

Required rate of return = 10%

Last dividend = $3.00

32. What is the yield to call on the following bond?

5 years remain until it can be called.

It is currently trading for $900.

The coupon payment is $90.

Call premium is 5%.

Par value is $1,000.

33. Calculate the weighted average cost of capital for a company with the following target capital structure and costs of capital.

Target capital structure: 50% debt, 10% preferred stock, 40% common equity

$K_d(1 - T) = 8.4\%$

$K_{ps} = 10.6\%$

$K_s = 13.75\%$

34. What is the internal rate of return of the following capital project?

Initial investment = $9,000

Cash flow in year 1 = $5,000

Cash flow in year 2 = $3,500

Cash flow in year 3 = $1,500

Cash flow in year 4 = $850

TEST YOURSELF

35. What are the annual cash flows for the following capital project to purchase new equipment?

New equipment cost (including shipping and handling)	$10,000
Change in net working capital	$6,000
Expected revenue	$8,000/year
Expenses	$3,000/year
MACRS depreciation rates:	
33% in year 1	
45% in year 2	
15% in year 3	
Tax rate	25%
Expected sale price at end of year 3	$600

OTHER IMPORTANT STUFF

Useful Phrases When Traveling in France

Je ne savais pas qu'elle était ta frangine!

I didn't know she's your sister!

Qu'est-ce que tu fous avec cette fourchette?

What are you doing with that fork?

T'as l'air d'un bon type, et si je connais les bons mecs, je sais bien que tu ne me toueras pas.

You seem to be a good guy, and if I know a good guy, I know you won't kill me.

Je suis australien. Moi, aussi, je déteste les américains.

I'm Australian. I hate Americans, too.

T'as raison. C'est le plus bel escalier que j'ai jamais vu.

You're right. It's the most beautiful stairway I've ever seen.

Mon père est plus riche que ton père. Mon père, il peut acheter ton père. Donnes-moi ton Capri Sun.

My dad is richer than your dad. My dad can buy your dad. Give me your Capri Sun.

How to Use Your Financial Calculator

Important keys

- ¢ **f, CLX**: Used to clear the register—use before every calculation
- ¢ **n**: The number of periods
- ¢ **i**: The interest rate
- ¢ **PV**: The present value
- ¢ **FV**: The future value
- ¢ **BEG or BGN**: Change to the beginning of the year. Use these for annuity due calculations. Sometimes you need to press g first.
- ¢ **CHS or** +/−: To make debits into negative numbers
- ¢ **g or COMP**: Used on some calculators to tell the calculator to calculate (if you want to know the future value, press COMP before FV).

Financial Calculator Practice

$ **Future Value Problem**

$2,000 has been deposited in a savings account at an interest rate of 10% per year for 3 years.

CALCULATION:

You Enter	You See	Why
3 n	3.00	enters the # of periods
1 0 i	10.00	enters the interest rate
2 0 0 0 PV	2,000.00	enters present value
FV	2,662.00	the answer

Remember, for semiannual, quarterly, or monthly compounding, multiply the number of periods by 2, 4, or 12, and divide the interest rate by the same number.

$ **Future Value of an Annuity**

$600 is deposited in the bank at the end of each year at 6% interest for 5 years.

CALCULATION:

You Enter	You See	Why
5 n	5.00	enters the # of periods
6 i	6.00	enters the interest rate
6 0 0 CHS PMT	−600.00	enters the payment
FV	3,382.26	the answer

Other Stuff

$ **Future Value of an Annuity Due**

$500 is deposited in the bank at the beginning of each year at 5% interest for 5 years.

CALCULATION:

You Enter	You See	Why
g BEG	BEGIN	changes to beginning of year
5 n	5.00	enters the # of periods
5 i	5.00	enters the interest rate
5 0 0 CHS PMT	−500.00	enters the payment
FV	2,900.96	present value

$ **Present Value**

How much would you deposit now at 5% to get $100,000 in 10 years?

CALCULATION:

You Enter	You See	Why
1 0 n	10.00	enters the # of periods
5 i	5.00	enters the interest rate
100000 CHS FV	−100,000	enters the future value
PV	38,554.33	the answer

$ Present Value of an Annuity

What's the worth of $1,000 payments for 10 years, if the market rate is 8%?

CALCULATION:

You Enter	You See	Why
1 0 n	10.00	enters the # of periods
8 i	8.00	enters the interest rate
1 0 0 0 CHS PMT	−1,000	enters the payment
PV	7246.89	the answer

"Make up your mind."

Igor

TABLE UNO FVIF

	1%	2%	3%	4%	5%	6%	7%	8%	9%	10%	11%	12%	13%	14%	15%	16%	17%	18%	19%	20%
1	1.010	1.020	1.030	1.040	1.050	1.060	1.070	1.080	1.090	1.100	1.110	1.120	1.130	1.140	1.150	1.160	1.170	1.180	1.190	1.200
2	1.020	1.040	1.061	1.082	1.103	1.124	1.145	1.166	1.188	1.210	1.232	1.254	1.277	1.300	1.323	1.346	1.369	1.392	1.416	1.440
3	1.030	1.061	1.093	1.125	1.158	1.191	1.225	1.260	1.295	1.331	1.368	1.405	1.443	1.482	1.521	1.561	1.602	1.643	1.685	1.728
4	1.041	1.082	1.126	1.170	1.216	1.262	1.311	1.360	1.412	1.464	1.518	1.574	1.630	1.689	1.749	1.811	1.874	1.939	2.005	2.074
5	1.051	1.104	1.159	1.217	1.276	1.338	1.403	1.469	1.539	1.611	1.685	1.762	1.842	1.925	2.011	2.100	2.192	2.288	2.386	2.488
6	1.062	1.126	1.194	1.265	1.340	1.419	1.501	1.587	1.677	1.772	1.870	1.974	2.082	2.195	2.313	2.436	2.565	2.700	2.840	2.986
7	1.072	1.149	1.230	1.316	1.407	1.504	1.606	1.714	1.828	1.949	2.076	2.211	2.353	2.502	2.660	2.826	3.001	3.185	3.379	3.583
8	1.083	1.172	1.267	1.369	1.477	1.594	1.718	1.851	1.993	2.144	2.305	2.476	2.658	2.853	3.059	3.278	3.511	3.759	4.021	4.300
9	1.094	1.195	1.305	1.423	1.551	1.689	1.838	1.999	2.172	2.358	2.558	2.773	3.004	3.252	3.518	3.803	4.108	4.435	4.785	5.160
10	1.105	1.219	1.344	1.480	1.629	1.791	1.967	2.159	2.367	2.594	2.839	3.106	3.395	3.707	4.046	4.411	4.807	5.234	5.695	6.192
11	1.116	1.243	1.384	1.539	1.710	1.898	2.105	2.332	2.580	2.853	3.152	3.479	3.836	4.226	4.652	5.117	5.624	6.176	6.777	7.430
12	1.127	1.268	1.426	1.601	1.796	2.012	2.252	2.518	2.813	3.138	3.498	3.896	4.335	4.818	5.350	5.936	6.580	7.288	8.064	8.916
13	1.138	1.294	1.469	1.665	1.886	2.133	2.410	2.720	3.066	3.452	3.883	4.363	4.898	5.492	6.153	6.886	7.699	8.599	9.596	10.699
14	1.149	1.319	1.513	1.732	1.980	2.261	2.579	2.937	3.342	3.797	4.310	4.887	5.535	6.261	7.076	7.988	9.007	10.147	11.420	12.839
15	1.161	1.346	1.558	1.801	2.079	2.397	2.759	3.172	3.642	4.177	4.785	5.474	6.254	7.138	8.137	9.266	10.539	11.974	13.590	15.407
16	1.173	1.373	1.605	1.873	2.183	2.540	2.952	3.426	3.970	4.595	5.311	6.130	7.067	8.137	9.358	10.748	12.330	14.129	16.172	18.488
17	1.184	1.400	1.653	1.948	2.292	2.693	3.159	3.700	4.328	5.054	5.895	6.866	7.986	9.276	10.761	12.468	14.426	16.672	19.244	22.186
18	1.196	1.428	1.702	2.026	2.407	2.854	3.380	3.996	4.717	5.560	6.544	7.690	9.024	10.575	12.375	14.463	16.879	19.673	22.901	26.623
19	1.208	1.457	1.754	2.107	2.527	3.026	3.617	4.316	5.142	6.116	7.263	8.613	10.197	12.056	14.232	16.777	19.748	23.214	27.252	31.948
20	1.220	1.486	1.806	2.191	2.653	3.207	3.870	4.661	5.604	6.727	8.062	9.646	11.523	13.743	16.367	19.461	23.106	27.393	32.429	38.338
21	1.232	1.516	1.860	2.279	2.786	3.400	4.141	5.034	6.109	7.400	8.949	10.804	13.021	15.668	18.822	22.574	27.034	32.324	38.591	46.005
22	1.245	1.546	1.916	2.370	2.925	3.604	4.430	5.437	6.659	8.140	9.934	12.100	14.714	17.861	21.645	26.186	31.629	38.142	45.923	55.206
23	1.257	1.577	1.974	2.465	3.072	3.820	4.741	5.871	7.258	8.954	11.026	13.552	16.627	20.362	24.891	30.376	37.006	45.008	54.649	66.247
24	1.270	1.608	2.033	2.563	3.225	4.049	5.072	6.341	7.911	9.850	12.239	15.179	18.788	23.212	28.625	35.236	43.297	53.109	65.032	79.497
25	1.282	1.641	2.094	2.666	3.386	4.292	5.427	6.848	8.623	10.835	13.585	17.000	21.231	26.462	32.919	40.874	50.658	62.669	77.388	95.396
26	1.295	1.673	2.157	2.772	3.556	4.549	5.807	7.396	9.399	11.918	15.080	19.040	23.991	30.167	37.857	47.414	59.270	73.949	92.092	114.475
27	1.308	1.707	2.221	2.883	3.733	4.822	6.214	7.988	10.245	13.110	16.739	21.32	27.109	34.390	43.535	55.000	69.345	87.260	109.589	137.371
28	1.321	1.741	2.288	2.999	3.920	5.112	6.649	8.627	11.167	14.421	18.580	23.88	30.633	39.204	50.066	63.800	81.134	102.967	130.411	164.845
29	1.335	1.776	2.357	3.119	4.116	5.418	7.114	9.317	12.172	15.863	20.62	26.75	34.616	44.693	57.575	74.009	94.927	121.501	155.189	197.814
30	1.348	1.811	2.427	3.243	4.322	5.743	7.612	10.063	13.268	17.449	22.89	29.96	39.116	50.950	66.212	85.850	111.065	143.371	184.675	237.376
35	1.417	2.000	2.814	3.946	5.516	7.686	10.677	14.785	20.414	28.102	38.575	52.800	72.069	98.100	133.176	180.314	243.50	328.00	440.70	590.67
40	1.489	2.208	3.262	4.801	7.040	10.286	14.974	21.725	31.409	45.259	65.001	93.051	132.782	188.88	267.86	378.72	533.87	750.38	1051.67	1469.8
45	1.565	2.438	3.782	5.841	8.985	13.765	21.002	31.920	48.327	72.890	109.53	163.99	244.64	363.68	538.77	795.44	1170.5	1716.7	2509.7	3657.3
50	1.645	2.692	4.384	7.107	11.467	18.420	29.457	46.902	74.358	117.391	184.56	289.00	450.74	700.23	1083.66	1670.7	2566.2	3927.4	5988.9	9100.4
55	1.729	2.972	5.082	8.646	14.636	24.650	41.315	68.914	114.408	189.059	311.00	509.32	830.5	1348.2	2179.6	3509.0	5626.3	8984.8	14291.7	

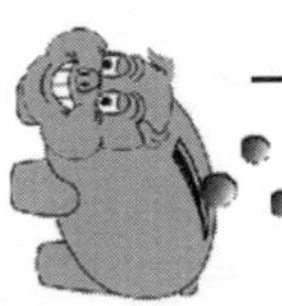

TABLE DOS FVIFA

	1%	2%	3%	4%	5%	6%	7%	8%	9%	10%	11%	12%	13%	14%	15%	16%	17%	18%	19%	20%
1	1.000	1.000	1.000	1.000	1.000	1.000	1.000	1.000	1.000	1.000	1.000	1.000	1.000	1.000	1.000	1.000	1.000	1.000	1.000	1.000
2	2.010	2.020	2.030	2.040	2.050	2.060	2.070	2.080	2.090	2.100	2.110	2.120	2.130	2.140	2.150	2.160	2.170	2.180	2.190	2.200
3	3.030	3.060	3.091	3.122	3.153	3.184	3.215	3.246	3.278	3.310	3.342	3.374	3.407	3.440	3.473	3.506	3.539	3.572	3.606	3.640
4	4.060	4.122	4.184	4.246	4.310	4.375	4.440	4.506	4.573	4.641	4.710	4.779	4.850	4.921	4.993	5.066	5.141	5.215	5.291	5.368
5	5.101	5.204	5.309	5.416	5.526	5.637	5.751	5.867	5.985	6.105	6.228	6.353	6.480	6.610	6.742	6.877	7.014	7.154	7.297	7.442
6	6.152	6.308	6.468	6.633	6.802	6.975	7.153	7.336	7.523	7.716	7.913	8.115	8.323	8.536	8.754	8.977	9.207	9.442	9.683	9.930
7	7.214	7.434	7.662	7.898	8.142	8.394	8.654	8.923	9.200	9.487	9.783	10.089	10.405	10.730	11.067	11.414	11.772	12.142	12.523	12.916
8	8.286	8.583	8.892	9.214	9.549	9.897	10.260	10.637	11.028	11.436	11.859	12.300	12.757	13.233	13.727	14.240	14.773	15.327	15.902	16.499
9	9.369	9.755	10.159	10.583	11.027	11.491	11.978	12.488	13.021	13.579	14.164	14.776	15.416	16.085	16.786	17.519	18.285	19.086	19.923	20.799
10	10.462	10.950	11.464	12.006	12.578	13.181	13.816	14.487	15.193	15.937	16.722	17.549	18.420	19.337	20.304	21.321	22.393	23.521	24.709	25.959
11	11.567	12.169	12.808	13.486	14.207	14.972	15.784	16.645	17.560	18.531	19.561	20.655	21.814	23.045	24.349	25.733	27.200	28.755	30.404	32.150
12	12.683	13.412	14.192	15.026	15.917	16.870	17.888	18.977	20.141	21.384	22.713	24.133	25.650	27.271	29.002	30.850	32.824	34.931	37.180	39.581
13	13.809	14.680	15.618	16.627	17.713	18.882	20.141	21.495	22.953	24.523	26.212	28.029	29.985	32.089	34.352	36.786	39.404	42.219	45.244	48.497
14	14.947	15.974	17.086	18.292	19.599	21.015	22.550	24.215	26.019	27.975	30.095	32.393	34.883	37.581	40.505	43.672	47.103	50.818	54.841	59.196
15	16.097	17.293	18.599	20.024	21.579	23.276	25.129	27.152	29.361	31.772	34.405	37.280	40.417	43.842	47.580	51.660	56.110	60.965	66.261	72.035
16	17.258	18.639	20.157	21.825	23.657	25.673	27.888	30.324	33.003	35.950	39.190	42.753	46.672	50.980	55.717	60.925	66.649	72.939	79.850	87.442
17	18.430	20.012	21.762	23.698	25.840	28.213	30.840	33.750	36.974	40.545	44.501	48.884	53.739	59.118	65.075	71.673	78.979	87.068	96.022	105.931
18	19.615	21.412	23.414	25.645	28.132	30.906	33.999	37.450	41.301	45.599	50.396	55.750	61.725	68.394	75.836	84.141	93.406	103.740	115.266	128.117
19	20.811	22.841	25.117	27.671	30.539	33.760	37.379	41.446	46.018	51.159	56.939	63.440	70.749	78.969	88.212	98.603	110.285	123.414	138.166	154.740
20	22.019	24.297	26.870	29.778	33.066	36.786	40.995	45.762	51.160	57.275	64.203	72.052	80.947	91.025	102.444	115.380	130.033	146.628	165.418	186.688
21	23.239	25.783	28.676	31.969	35.719	39.993	44.865	50.423	56.765	64.002	72.265	81.699	92.47	104.77	118.81	134.84	153.14	174.02	197.85	225.03
22	24.472	27.299	30.537	34.248	38.505	43.392	49.006	55.457	62.873	71.403	81.214	92.503	105.49	120.44	137.63	157.41	180.17	206.34	236.44	271.03
23	25.716	28.845	32.453	36.618	41.430	46.996	53.436	60.893	69.532	79.543	91.148	104.603	120.20	138.30	159.28	183.60	211.80	244.49	282.36	326.24
24	26.973	30.422	34.426	39.083	44.502	50.816	58.177	66.765	76.790	88.497	102.174	118.155	136.83	158.66	184.17	213.98	248.81	289.49	337.01	392.48
25	28.243	32.030	36.459	41.646	47.727	54.865	63.249	73.106	84.701	98.347	114.413	133.334	155.62	181.87	212.79	249.21	292.10	342.60	402.04	471.98
26	29.526	33.671	38.553	44.312	51.113	59.156	68.676	79.954	93.324	109.182	127.999	150.334	176.85	208.33	245.71	290.09	342.76	405.27	479.43	567.38
27	30.821	35.344	40.710	47.084	54.669	63.706	74.484	87.351	102.723	121.100	143.079	169.374	200.84	238.50	283.57	337.50	402.03	479.22	571.52	681.85
28	32.129	37.051	42.931	49.968	58.403	68.528	80.698	95.339	112.968	134.210	159.817	190.699	227.95	272.89	327.10	392.50	471.38	566.48	681.11	819.22
29	33.450	38.792	45.219	52.966	62.323	73.640	87.347	103.966	124.135	148.631	178.397	214.583	258.58	312.09	377.17	456.30	552.51	669.45	811.52	984.07
30	34.785	40.568	47.575	56.085	66.439	79.058	94.461	113.283	136.308	164.494	199.021	241.333	293.2	356.8	434.7	530.3	647.4	790.9	966.7	1181.9
35	41.66	49.99	60.46	73.65	90.32	111.43	138.24	172.32	215.71	271.02	341.59	431.66	546.68	693.57	881.17	1120.7	1426.5	1816.7	2314.2	2948.3
40	48.89	60.40	75.40	95.03	120.80	154.76	199.64	259.06	337.88	442.59	581.83	767.09	1013.70	1342.03	1779.09	2360.8	3134.5	4163.2	5529.8	7343.9
45	56.48	71.89	92.72	121.03	159.70	212.74	285.75	386.51	525.86	718.90	986.64	1358.2	1874.2	2590.6	3585.1	4965.3	6879.3	9531.6	13203.4	18281.3
50	64.46	84.58	112.80	152.67	209.35	290.34	406.53	573.77	815.08	1163.9	1668.8	2400.0	3459.5	4994.5	7217.7	10435.6	15089.5	21813.1	31515.3	45497.2
55	72.85	98.59	136.07	191.16	272.71	394.17	575.93	848.92	1260.1	1880.6	2818.2	4236.0	6380.4	9623.1	14524.1	21925.3	33090.0	49910.2	75214.0	

TABLE TRES PVIF

	1%	2%	3%	4%	5%	6%	7%	8%	9%	10%	11%	12%	13%	14%	15%	16%	17%	18%	19%	20%
1	.9901	.9804	.9709	.9615	.9524	.9434	.9346	.9259	.9174	.9091	.9009	.8929	.8850	.8772	.8696	.8621	.8547	.8475	.8403	.8333
2	.9803	.9612	.9426	.9246	.9070	.8900	.8734	.8573	.8417	.8264	.8116	.7972	.7831	.7695	.7561	.7432	.7305	.7182	.7062	.6944
3	.9706	.9423	.9151	.8890	.8638	.8396	.8163	.7938	.7722	.7513	.7312	.7118	.6931	.6750	.6575	.6407	.6244	.6086	.5934	.5787
4	.9610	.9238	.8885	.8548	.8227	.7921	.7629	.7350	.7084	.6830	.6587	.6355	.6133	.5921	.5718	.5523	.5337	.5158	.4987	.4823
5	.9515	.9057	.8626	.8219	.7835	.7473	.7130	.6806	.6499	.6209	.5935	.5674	.5428	.5194	.4972	.4761	.4561	.4371	.4190	.4019
6	.9420	.8880	.8375	.7903	.7462	.7050	.6663	.6302	.5963	.5645	.5346	.5066	.4803	.4556	.4323	.4104	.3898	.3704	.3521	.3349
7	.9327	.8706	.8131	.7599	.7107	.6651	.6227	.5835	.5470	.5132	.4817	.4523	.4251	.3996	.3759	.3538	.3332	.3139	.2959	.2791
8	.9235	.8535	.7894	.7307	.6768	.6274	.5820	.5403	.5019	.4665	.4339	.4039	.3762	.3506	.3269	.3050	.2848	.2660	.2487	.2326
9	.9143	.8368	.7664	.7026	.6446	.5919	.5439	.5002	.4604	.4241	.3909	.3606	.3329	.3075	.2843	.2630	.2434	.2255	.2090	.1938
10	.9053	.8203	.7441	.6756	.6139	.5584	.5083	.4632	.4224	.3855	.3522	.3220	.2946	.2697	.2472	.2267	.2080	.1911	.1756	.1615
11	.8963	.8043	.7224	.6496	.5847	.5268	.4751	.4289	.3875	.3505	.3173	.2875	.2607	.2366	.2149	.1954	.1778	.1619	.1476	.1346
12	.8874	.7885	.7014	.6246	.5568	.4970	.4440	.3971	.3555	.3186	.2858	.2567	.2307	.2076	.1869	.1685	.1520	.1372	.1240	.1122
13	.8787	.7730	.6810	.6006	.5303	.4688	.4150	.3677	.3262	.2897	.2575	.2292	.2042	.1821	.1625	.1452	.1299	.1163	.1042	.0935
14	.8700	.7579	.6611	.5775	.5051	.4423	.3878	.3405	.2992	.2633	.2320	.2046	.1807	.1597	.1413	.1252	.1110	.0985	.0876	.0779
15	.8613	.7430	.6419	.5553	.4810	.4173	.3624	.3152	.2745	.2394	.2090	.1827	.1599	.1401	.1229	.1079	.0949	.0835	.0736	.0649
16	.8528	.7284	.6232	.5339	.4581	.3936	.3387	.2919	.2519	.2176	.1883	.1631	.1415	.1229	.1069	.0930	.0811	.0708	.0618	.0541
17	.8444	.7142	.6050	.5134	.4363	.3714	.3166	.2703	.2311	.1978	.1696	.1456	.1252	.1078	.0929	.0802	.0693	.0600	.0520	.0451
18	.8360	.7002	.5874	.4936	.4155	.3503	.2959	.2502	.2120	.1799	.1528	.1300	.1108	.0946	.0808	.0691	.0592	.0508	.0437	.0376
19	.8277	.6864	.5703	.4746	.3957	.3305	.2765	.2317	.1945	.1635	.1377	.1161	.0981	.0829	.0703	.0596	.0506	.0431	.0367	.0313
20	.8195	.6730	.5537	.4564	.3769	.3118	.2584	.2145	.1784	.1486	.1240	.1037	.0868	.0728	.0611	.0514	.0433	.0365	.0308	.0261
21	.8114	.6598	.5375	.4388	.3589	.2942	.2415	.1987	.1637	.1351	.1117	.0926	.0768	.0638	.0531	.0443	.0370	.0309	.0259	.0217
22	.8034	.6468	.5219	.4220	.3418	.2775	.2257	.1839	.1502	.1228	.1007	.0826	.0680	.0560	.0462	.0382	.0316	.0262	.0218	.0181
23	.7954	.6342	.5067	.4057	.3256	.2618	.2109	.1703	.1378	.1117	.0907	.0738	.0601	.0491	.0402	.0329	.0270	.0222	.0183	.0151
24	.7876	.6217	.4919	.3901	.3101	.2470	.1971	.1577	.1264	.1015	.0817	.0659	.0532	.0431	.0349	.0284	.0231	.0188	.0154	.0126
25	.7798	.6095	.4776	.3751	.2953	.2330	.1842	.1460	.1160	.0923	.0736	.0588	.0471	.0378	.0304	.0245	.0197	.0160	.0129	.0105
26	.7720	.5976	.4637	.3607	.2812	.2198	.1722	.1352	.1064	.0839	.0663	.0525	.0417	.0331	.0264	.0211	.0169	.0135	.0109	.0087
27	.7644	.5859	.4502	.3468	.2678	.2074	.1609	.1252	.0976	.0763	.0597	.0469	.0369	.0291	.0230	.0182	.0144	.0115	.0091	.0073
28	.7568	.5744	.4371	.3335	.2551	.1956	.1504	.1159	.0895	.0693	.0538	.0419	.0326	.0255	.0200	.0157	.0123	.0097	.0077	.0061
29	.7493	.5631	.4243	.3207	.2429	.1846	.1406	.1073	.0822	.0630	.0485	.0374	.0289	.0224	.0174	.0135	.0105	.0082	.0064	.0051
30	.7419	.5521	.4120	.3083	.2314	.1741	.1314	.0994	.0754	.0573	.0437	.0334	.0256	.0196	.0151	.0116	.0090	.0070	.0054	.0042
35	.7059	.5000	.3554	.2534	.1813	.1301	.0937	.0676	.0490	.0356	.0259	.0189	.0139	.0102	.0075	.0055	.0041	.0030	.0023	.0017
40	.6717	.4529	.3066	.2083	.1420	.0972	.0668	.0460	.0318	.0221	.0154	.0107	.0075	.0053	.0037	.0026	.0019	.0013	.0010	.0007
45	.6391	.4102	.2644	.1712	.1113	.0727	.0476	.0313	.0207	.0137	.0091	.0061	.0041	.0027	.0019	.0013	.0009	.0006	.0004	.0003
50	.6080	.3715	.2281	.1407	.0872	.0543	.0339	.0213	.0134	.0085	.0054	.0035	.0022	.0014	.0009	.0006	.0004	.0003	.0002	.0001
55	.5785	.3365	.1968	.1157	.0683	.0406	.0242	.0145	.0087	.0053	.0032	.0020	.0012	.0007	.0005	.0003	.0002	.0001	.0001	.0000

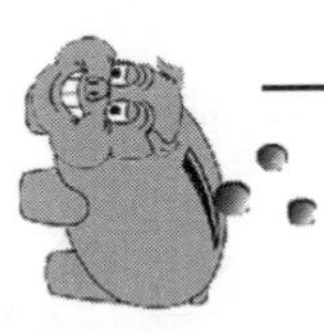

TABLE QUATRO PVIFA

	1%	2%	3%	4%	5%	6%	7%	8%	9%	10%	11%	12%	13%	14%	15%	16%	17%	18%	19%	20%
1	.9901	.9804	.9709	.9615	.9524	.9434	.9346	.9259	.9174	.9091	.9009	.8929	.8850	.8772	.8696	.8621	.8547	.8475	.8403	.8333
2	1.9704	1.9416	1.9135	1.8861	1.8594	1.8334	1.8080	1.7833	1.7591	1.7355	1.7125	1.6901	1.6681	1.6467	1.6257	1.6052	1.5852	1.5656	1.5465	1.5278
3	2.9410	2.8839	2.8286	2.7751	2.7232	2.6730	2.6243	2.5771	2.5313	2.4869	2.4437	2.4018	2.3612	2.3216	2.2832	2.2459	2.2096	2.1743	2.1399	2.1065
4	3.9020	3.8077	3.7171	3.6299	3.5460	3.4651	3.3872	3.3121	3.2397	3.1699	3.1024	3.0373	2.9745	2.9137	2.8550	2.7982	2.7432	2.6901	2.6386	2.5887
5	4.8534	4.7135	4.5797	4.4518	4.3295	4.2124	4.1002	3.9927	3.8897	3.7908	3.6959	3.6048	3.5172	3.4331	3.3522	3.2743	3.1993	3.1272	3.0576	2.9906
6	5.7955	5.6014	5.4172	5.2421	5.0757	4.9173	4.7665	4.6229	4.4859	4.3553	4.2305	4.1114	3.9975	3.8887	3.7845	3.6847	3.5892	3.4976	3.4098	3.3255
7	6.7282	6.4720	6.2303	6.0021	5.7864	5.5824	5.3893	5.2064	5.0330	4.8684	4.7122	4.5638	4.4226	4.2883	4.1604	4.0386	3.9224	3.8115	3.7057	3.6046
8	7.6517	7.3255	7.0197	6.7327	6.4632	6.2098	5.9713	5.7466	5.5348	5.3349	5.1461	4.9676	4.7988	4.6389	4.4873	4.3436	4.2072	4.0776	3.9544	3.8372
9	8.5660	8.1622	7.7861	7.4353	7.1078	6.8017	6.5152	6.2469	5.9952	5.7590	5.5370	5.3282	5.1317	4.9464	4.7716	4.6065	4.4506	4.3030	4.1633	4.0310
10	9.4713	8.9826	8.5302	8.1109	7.7217	7.3601	7.0236	6.7101	6.4177	6.1446	5.8892	5.6502	5.4262	5.2161	5.0188	4.8332	4.6586	4.4941	4.3389	4.1925
11	10.3676	9.7868	9.2526	8.7605	8.3064	7.8869	7.4987	7.1390	6.8052	6.4951	6.2065	5.9377	5.6869	5.4527	5.2337	5.0286	4.8364	4.6560	4.4865	4.3271
12	11.2551	10.5753	9.9540	9.3851	8.8633	8.3838	7.9427	7.5361	7.1607	6.8137	6.4924	6.1944	5.9176	5.6603	5.4206	5.1971	4.9884	4.7932	4.6105	4.4392
13	12.1337	11.3484	10.6350	9.9856	9.3936	8.8527	8.3577	7.9038	7.4869	7.1034	6.7499	6.4235	6.1218	5.8424	5.5831	5.3423	5.1183	4.9095	4.7147	4.5327
14	13.0037	12.1062	11.2961	10.5631	9.8986	9.2950	8.7455	8.2442	7.7862	7.3667	6.9819	6.6282	6.3025	6.0021	5.7245	5.4675	5.2293	5.0081	4.8023	4.6106
15	13.8651	12.8493	11.9379	11.1184	10.3797	9.7122	9.1079	8.5595	8.0607	7.6061	7.1909	6.8109	6.4624	6.1422	5.8474	5.5755	5.3242	5.0916	4.8759	4.6755
16	14.7179	13.5777	12.5611	11.6523	10.8378	10.1059	9.4466	8.8514	8.3126	7.8237	7.3792	6.9740	6.6039	6.2651	5.9542	5.6685	5.4053	5.1624	4.9377	4.7296
17	15.5623	14.2919	13.1661	12.1657	11.2741	10.4773	9.7632	9.1216	8.5436	8.0216	7.5488	7.1196	6.7291	6.3729	6.0472	5.7487	5.4746	5.2223	4.9897	4.7746
18	16.3983	14.9920	13.7535	12.6593	11.6896	10.8276	10.0591	9.3719	8.7556	8.2014	7.7016	7.2497	6.8399	6.4674	6.1280	5.8178	5.5339	5.2732	5.0333	4.8122
19	17.2260	15.6785	14.3238	13.1339	12.0853	11.1581	10.3356	9.6036	8.9501	8.3649	7.8393	7.3658	6.9380	6.5504	6.1982	5.8775	5.5845	5.3162	5.0700	4.8435
20	18.0456	16.3514	14.8775	13.5903	12.4622	11.4699	10.5940	9.8181	9.1285	8.5136	7.9633	7.4694	7.0248	6.6231	6.2593	5.9288	5.6278	5.3527	5.1009	4.8696
21	18.8570	17.0112	15.4150	14.0292	12.8212	11.7641	10.8355	10.0168	9.2922	8.6487	8.0751	7.5620	7.1016	6.6870	6.3125	5.9731	5.6648	5.3837	5.1268	4.8913
22	19.6604	17.6580	15.9369	14.4511	13.1630	12.0416	11.0612	10.2007	9.4424	8.7715	8.1757	7.6446	7.1695	6.7429	6.3587	6.0113	5.6964	5.4099	5.1486	4.9094
23	20.4558	18.2922	16.4436	14.8568	13.4886	12.3034	11.2722	10.3711	9.5802	8.8832	8.2664	7.7184	7.2297	6.7921	6.3988	6.0442	5.7234	5.4321	5.1668	4.9245
24	21.2434	18.9139	16.9355	15.2470	13.7986	12.5504	11.4693	10.5288	9.7066	8.9847	8.3481	7.7843	7.2829	6.8351	6.4338	6.0726	5.7465	5.4509	5.1822	4.9371
25	22.0232	19.5235	17.4131	15.6221	14.0939	12.7834	11.6536	10.6748	9.8226	9.0770	8.4217	7.8431	7.3300	6.8729	6.4641	6.0971	5.7662	5.4669	5.1951	4.9476
26	22.7952	20.1210	17.8768	15.9828	14.3752	13.0032	11.8258	10.8100	9.9290	9.1609	8.4881	7.8957	7.3717	6.9061	6.4906	6.1182	5.7831	5.4804	5.2060	4.9563
27	23.5596	20.7069	18.3270	16.3296	14.6430	13.2105	11.9867	10.9352	10.0266	9.2372	8.5478	7.9426	7.4086	6.9352	6.5135	6.1364	5.7975	5.4919	5.2151	4.9636
28	24.3164	21.2813	18.7641	16.6631	14.8981	13.4062	12.1371	11.0511	10.1161	9.3066	8.6016	7.9844	7.4412	6.9607	6.5335	6.1520	5.8099	5.5016	5.2228	4.9697
29	25.0658	21.8444	19.1885	16.9837	15.1411	13.5907	12.2777	11.1584	10.1983	9.3696	8.6501	8.0218	7.4701	6.9830	6.5509	6.1656	5.8204	5.5098	5.2292	4.9747
30	25.8077	22.3965	19.6004	17.2920	15.3725	13.7648	12.4090	11.2578	10.2737	9.4269	8.6938	8.0552	7.4957	7.0027	6.5660	6.1772	5.8294	5.5168	5.2347	4.9789
35	29.4086	24.9986	21.4872	18.6646	16.3742	14.4982	12.9477	11.6546	10.5668	9.6442	8.8552	8.1755	7.5856	7.0700	6.6166	6.2153	5.8582	5.5386	5.2512	4.9915
40	32.8347	27.3555	23.1148	19.7928	17.1591	15.0463	13.3317	11.9246	10.7574	9.7791	8.9511	8.2438	7.6344	7.1050	6.6418	6.2335	5.8713	5.5482	5.2582	4.9966
45	36.0945	29.4902	24.5187	20.7200	17.7741	15.4558	13.6055	12.1084	10.8812	9.8628	9.0079	8.2825	7.6609	7.1232	6.6543	6.2421	5.8773	5.5523	5.2611	4.9986
50	39.1961	31.4236	25.7298	21.4822	18.2559	15.7619	13.8007	12.2335	10.9617	9.9148	9.0417	8.3045	7.6752	7.1327	6.6605	6.2463	5.8801	5.5541	5.2623	4.9995
55	42.1472	33.1748	26.7744	22.1086	18.6335	15.9905	13.9399	12.3186	11.0140	9.9471	9.0617	8.3170	7.6830	7.1376	6.6636	6.2482	5.8813	5.5549	5.2628	4.9998

Formulas Part 1

Future Value:

$$FV = PV(FVIF)$$

Future Value of an Annuity

$$FV = PAY(FVIFA)$$

Present Value:

$$PV = FV(PVIF)$$

Present Value of an Annuity

$$PV = PAY(PVIFA)$$

Present Value of a Perpetuity

$$PV = \frac{PAY}{i}$$

Effective Annual Rate

$$EAR = \left(1 + \frac{i}{m}\right)^m - 1$$

The Master Formula for Compounding

$$FV = PV\left(1 + \frac{i}{m}\right)^{mn}$$

Expected Rate of Return

$$\hat{K} = P_1(\text{Outcome}_1) + P_2(\text{Outcome}_2) + P_3(\text{Outcome}_3)$$

Standard Deviation of a Stock

$$\sigma = \sqrt{\Sigma(K_i - \hat{K})^2 P_i}$$

Coefficient of Variation

$$CV = \frac{\sigma}{\hat{K}}$$

Formulas Part 2

Expected Rate of Return on a Portfolio

$$\hat{K}_p = W_1K_1 + W_2K_2 + W_3K_3$$

Capital Asset Pricing Model (CAP-M)

$$K_s = K_{RF} + b(K_M - K_{RF})$$

OTHER STUFF

Bond Current Price:

BPV = Coupon Payment(PVIFA) + Par Value(PVIF)

Discount or Premium:

(Old Pay − New Pay) × (PVIFA[new rate and period])

Bond Current Yield:

$$\text{Current yield} = \frac{\text{Interest Pay}}{\text{Bond PV}}$$

Present Value of a Preferred Stock:

$$k_p = \frac{D}{PV}$$

Present Value of a Normal Growth Stock:

(Gordon Growth Model)

$$P_0 = \frac{D_1}{K_s - g} \qquad \text{where } D_1 = D_0(1 + g)$$

Present Value of a Differential (supernormal) Growth Stock:

1. PV of Dividends
2. Apply Constant Growth Formula

$$P_0 = \frac{D_1}{K_s - g}$$

3. Discount Normal Growth Value
4. Discount Supernormal Dividends. Add dividends to present value of normal growth stock.

Formulas Part 3

Cost of Debt:

K_d = (interest rate on debt)(1-T)

Cost of Preferred Stock

$$K_{ps} = \frac{D_{ps}}{P_n}$$

Cost of Retained Earnings:

using CAPM: $K_s = K_{rf} + b(Km - K_{rf})$

using Bond-yield-plus-risk-premium: $i + [3 - 5]$

using DCF: $K_s = \frac{\text{DIV}}{\text{price}} + g$

Other Stuff

Cost of New Common Stock:

$$K_e = \frac{D_e}{P_e}(1 - F) + g$$

Weighted Average Cost of Capital:

$WACC = W_d K_d(1 - T) + W_{ps} K_{ps} + W_{ce} K_{re}$

(using retained earnings)

$WACC = W_d K_d(1 - T) + W_{ps} K_{ps} + W_{ce} K_e$

(using new common stock)

How to Do a Capital Budget:

1. Determine the cost of the project.
2. Estimate the expected cash flows the project will create.
3. Estimate the riskiness of the projected cash flows.
4. Determine the cost of capital at which the cash flows should be discounted.
5. Estimate the revenues of the project to the business by using the expected cash flows to calculate a present value.
6. Apply decision method to accept or reject project.

STRESSRELIEF

AND THIS IS NO LAUGHING MATTER.

The Finance Choose Your Own Adventure!

Start Here

1. It was early yesterday when your uncle sent you out on an important mission.

"Take this, my favorite business calculator, and find the mightiest stock in the market. Slay the beast and return it to me," he said.

So off you went, searching for the mightiest stock in the market. However, you had no clue where to look, so you spent the day wandering up and down Fifth Avenue. At noon, you stopped and had some pizza and a soda. At six, you went to Roxy Deli and used your uncle's credit card to order a sandwich larger than your own head. A bit bloated, you retired to a brownstone in the Village. You're not sure whose brownstone it was, but they didn't seem to mind.

So it's a new day, and you need to get cracking. Where do you want to start?

The World Trade Center? Turn to #2.

Wall Street? Go to #3.

The Statue of Liberty? Skip to #4.

2. You decide to go to the World Trade Center. You're not sure what they trade there, but "trading" does imply "market," and that's where your uncle said to find the mightiest stock.

But the World Trade Center is far from where you are now, and you don't have a glider. You decide to take the crosstown bus.

On the bus, you sit across from a man who clears his throat every 15 seconds, and smells strongly of urine.

He stares at you for a while and then says:

"You wanna help me take a bath?" Then he wiggles his eyebrows suggestively.

What do you do?

Wash the man. Go to #7.

Scream and run. Go to #5.

Challenge him to a battle to the death. Go to #6.

3. You take a cab to Wall Street. When you get there, a young stockbroker walks up to you.

"I can't help but notice your beautiful calculator," she says, admiring your uncle's calculator.

"I'm looking for the mightiest stock in the market," you reply.

"I will trade you the mightiest stock in the market for your calculator," she says.

You think long and hard. As you're thinking, the stockbroker gets bored and begins to wander away. Panicked, you chase after her. There's no way you're gonna let this one get away!

She walks toward a revolving door leading into some skyscraper. You sprint into the street, hoping to catch her before she goes inside. Unfortunately, you don't see the crosstown bus hurtling toward you.

You expect to hear a smash when the bus hits you, but the sound is more like "squoop."

So there you lie, dying, and everyone gets off the bus to examine the carnage. Among the onlookers is a smelly man with respiratory problems and some weirdo with a financial calculator.

You expire. Messily.

The End.

4. You decide to go to the Statue of Liberty. You figure that the best place to find the mightiest stock in the market is also where you find the mightiest statue in the harbor.

You hail a cab and ask the driver to take you to the Statue of Liberty. The driver laughs evilly. You dismiss it as excessive mood-setting by the author.

You decide to read the newspaper during the ride, picking up a *New York Times* that spontaneously appeared next to you sometime during the last paragraph.

You just finish reading a story about a brownstone burglary in the Village when you notice something wrong. The cab seems to be going the wrong way!

"Hey!" you shout to the cabbie. He only laughs. Frantically, you look out the window. Where are you going?!! Too late, you realize — Jersey.

There is no escape from the black hole that is Jersey.

The End.

5. The smelly man frightens you too much. You scream and run for the side door of the bus, which for some reason is open, even though the bus is moving.

You fall roughly to the street, but feel okay. You look around to catch your breath and figure out where you are. Hmm. You're in Central Park.

Turn to #8.

6. You challenge the smelly man to combat. With lightning quickness you each draw your sword and fence across the back of the bus. On and on the battle rages. Eventually, you and the smelly man grow tired, yet you continue to swing at him and he at you.

The time reaches 9 pm. Still you fight. The bus nears Central Park and you falter. The smelly man seizes an opportunity and twists your sword out of your hand, flinging it out of the window. You watch the sword fly away from the bus. Straight and true, the sword flies directly toward some freak with a financial calculator who's sitting on a park bench. The sword impales him, and he looks down in surprise. In the meantime, the smelly man has been busily cutting you to pieces.

You expire. Messily.

The End.

7. You decide to help wash the man. At the next stop, the two of you get off the bus and climb into a fountain.

A few hours later you're both clean as a whistle.

"Thank you," says the formerly smelly man. Out of gratitude, he gives you his most valued possession: the mightiest stock in the market.

"This is just what I was looking for!" you exclaim.

"Me too," says the formerly smelly man.

You both return to your uncle's house, where he is so happy, he buys you both new shoes.

The End.

8. Central Park is nice this time of year so you decide to spend some time there. This whole stock thing can wait until tomorrow.

During the day, you meet a policeman on a horse, a really nice man named Napoleon, and two college students from Denmark. But time goes quickly, and before you know it, it's 9 pm. You sit on a bench to think things out.

Suddenly, you see something moving in front of you. Just as you look up, a sword comes flying out of a bus, and plants itself firmly in your chest.

Unable to conceal your surprise, you expire. Messily.

The End.

Fino Searcho

<table>
<tr><td>Y</td><td>C</td><td>A</td><td>N</td><td>N</td><td>U</td><td>I</td><td>T</td><td>Y</td><td>O</td><td>G</td><td>O</td><td>H</td><td>R</td></tr>
<tr><td>T</td><td>O</td><td>I</td><td>T</td><td>S</td><td>E</td><td>R</td><td>E</td><td>T</td><td>N</td><td>I</td><td>K</td><td>E</td><td>H</td></tr>
<tr><td>I</td><td>R</td><td>D</td><td>N</td><td>E</td><td>D</td><td>I</td><td>V</td><td>I</td><td>D</td><td>Y</td><td>K</td><td>N</td><td>Y</td></tr>
<tr><td>L</td><td>P</td><td>E</td><td>T</td><td>U</td><td>S</td><td>T</td><td>D</td><td>L</td><td>T</td><td>O</td><td>O</td><td>S</td><td>T</td></tr>
<tr><td>I</td><td>O</td><td>T</td><td>A</td><td>I</td><td>E</td><td>N</td><td>T</td><td>I</td><td>R</td><td>I</td><td>A</td><td>I</td><td>Y</td></tr>
<tr><td>B</td><td>R</td><td>N</td><td>B</td><td>S</td><td>U</td><td>T</td><td>U</td><td>B</td><td>T</td><td>T</td><td>O</td><td>C</td><td>I</td></tr>
<tr><td>A</td><td>A</td><td>A</td><td>S</td><td>O</td><td>U</td><td>T</td><td>E</td><td>A</td><td>E</td><td>I</td><td>T</td><td>A</td><td>E</td></tr>
<tr><td>I</td><td>T</td><td>A</td><td>P</td><td>I</td><td>E</td><td>R</td><td>L</td><td>B</td><td>L</td><td>P</td><td>E</td><td>P</td><td>L</td></tr>
<tr><td>L</td><td>I</td><td>M</td><td>C</td><td>P</td><td>A</td><td>F</td><td>E</td><td>O</td><td>U</td><td>U</td><td>E</td><td>I</td><td>D</td></tr>
<tr><td>G</td><td>O</td><td>I</td><td>R</td><td>S</td><td>N</td><td>T</td><td>F</td><td>R</td><td>K</td><td>C</td><td>O</td><td>T</td><td>S</td></tr>
<tr><td>C</td><td>N</td><td>E</td><td>E</td><td>I</td><td>A</td><td>T</td><td>K</td><td>P</td><td>T</td><td>S</td><td>F</td><td>A</td><td>H</td></tr>
<tr><td>G</td><td>P</td><td>C</td><td>R</td><td>R</td><td>R</td><td>N</td><td>E</td><td>B</td><td>H</td><td>K</td><td>I</td><td>L</td><td>N</td></tr>
<tr><td>C</td><td>A</td><td>I</td><td>I</td><td>O</td><td>A</td><td>L</td><td>E</td><td>J</td><td>A</td><td>N</td><td>D</td><td>R</td><td>O</td></tr>
<tr><td>R</td><td>R</td><td>P</td><td>P</td><td>B</td><td>E</td><td>D</td><td>N</td><td>O</td><td>B</td><td>S</td><td>T</td><td>I</td><td>R</td></tr>
</table>

ALEJANDRO, ANNUITY, ASSET, BANKRUPTCY, BETA, BOND, BROKER, CAPITAL, COMPOUNDING, CORPORATION, DEBT, DIVIDEND, ERASECAR, ICING, INFLATION, INTEREST, KILN, LIABILITY, PERPETUITY, PIRATE, PORTFOLIO, PROBABILITY, RISK, STIR, STOCK, TABIS, TREASURER, YIELD

Fino Crosso

ACROSS
6 Folder
8 Chance of bad stuff happening
9 Porter and Lager
14 Internal rate of return
15 Top-of-the-line
16 To fill
18 Playthings
21 A small, monkeylike demon
23 Money a company uses to do stuff
27 Something of value
29 Modified internal rate of return
32 The tendency of prices to rise over time
33 A hockey stick; a small branch

DOWN
1 Small, rubber racer
2 Interest on interest
3 Stuff that you owe
4 The antecedent of alpha
5 Bonds
6 An annuity that never ends
7 The inability to pay bills
10 Big oven for baking ceramics
11 Symbolic cost of wear and tear on stuff
12 A steady stream of equal payments
13 Capital asset pricing model
17 An entity created to do business
19 To surrender
20 Less than full price
22 Savings ________
23 Joe
24 Money keep-tracker
25 A fee charged for the use of money
26 Stuff you chew
28 Nigiri and maki
30 Hockey violation
31 Weighted average cost of capital

THE ANSWER MAN

The Answer Man is dedicated to alleviating the worries of his fellow Cerebellum employees. Each day, he receives hundreds of letters from coworkers. We have reprinted some of them here, along with the Answer Man's responses. We hope they will be helpful to you, too.

Dear Answer Man:

If those guys got forty years in prison for stealing stop signs, what would happen if I went out one night and put up stop signs?

That's easy. People would be stopping more often and in random places.

Dear Answer Man:

Does the government have anything to do with the pronunciation of February as "Febuairy"? If not, who does?

A very insightful question. Documents recently released by the CIA indicate that in 1966 the U.S. Government had nothing to do with the pronunciation of February. **This incident, referred to as** The Basketball Game, **changed** absolutely nothing **forever. With this evidence, we can be sure that the government is** no **more involved in our lives than ever before.**

THE ANSWER MAN

Dear Answer Man:

If I plant hamburger meat in my garden in April and water it every day, will I have a cow in November?

No. You'll have maggots. Remember that scene from Poltergeist? Yuck.

Dear Answer Man:
Why do people speak different languages? Don't give me the biblical reason either, that's a load of hooey.

In case you haven't noticed, every language is WRITTEN differently. You can't pronounce Guenoc the same way you say Jewarhelol. People are just dealing with what they're given. Incidentally, languages are written differently because everyone has a different way of holding a pen.

"I shall tell you a great secret, my friend. Do not wait for the last judgment. It takes place every day."

Albert Camus

Dear Answer Man:

You are a great help to me. Please, answer two more questions for me.

- How can you know your true nature from the sound of a cricket's chirping?
- What is the sound of one hand clapping?
- What is the linguistic root of fuschia?

STUDY SIDEKICK

The Answer Man is happy to answer your questions. It is not easy to discover your nature through the chirp of a cricket, but I offer this advice:

Study hard.

Listen to the cricket.

Lather.

Rinse.

Repeat as necessary.

The sound of one hand clapping is none, because no one is in the forest to hear it. The linguistic root of fuschia: from the Latin, fuscus, which means "dark brown."

By the way, you asked three questions. Learn how to count, muttonhead.

Dear Answer Man:

How come you got all the answers?

None of your business, jerk.

Do YOU have a question for the Answer Man? Send your questions about life, love, and the world in general to:

The Answer Man
2890 Emma Street
Fairfax, VA 22402

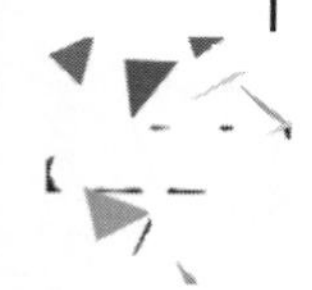

THE ANSWERS

Quiz 1

1. maximize stockholder wealth
2. sole proprietorship, partnership, corporation
3. taxes, personal liability
4. sole proprietorship, partnership
5. limited partners
6. shareholders or stockholders
7. investors are not personally liable, ease of shifting ownership, never dies
8. earnings per share or EPS
9. earnings per share
10. any three of the following: projected earnings per share of stock, amount of future risk, amount of corporate debt, dividend policy of the corporation, or perceived ability to generate profit over time
11. retained earnings
12. board of directors, shareholders
13. agency problems
14. T-account
15. annual report
16. preferred
17. income statement

18. K
19. real rate, inflation premium, risk premium
20. real rate, K*
21. risk premium
22. risk-free rate, K_{rf}
23. yield curves, upward
24. T-bill, T-note, T-bond
25. long term, short term

Quiz 2

1. future value
2. compounding
3. present value times one plus the interest rate raised to the nth power or [$FV = PV (1 + i)^n$]
4. FVIF, $(1 + i)^n$
5. divided by two, multiplied by two
6. annuity
7. annuity due
8. FVannuity = PAY (FVIFA)
9. FVannuity due = PAY (FVIFA) (1 + i)
10. present value
11. present value
12. $\left(\frac{1}{1} + i\right)n$
13. opportunity cost rate
14. PVA = PAY (PVIFA)

15. PVannuity due = PAY (PVIFA) (1 + i)
16. perpetuity
17. present value of a perpetuity
18. market or nominal rate
19. annual percentage rate, APR
20. periodic rate
21. effective annual rate, EAR
22. $FV = PV (1 + i/m)^{mn}$
23. cash flows
24. cash flows, future value
25. each and every, calculated separately, period, totaled together

Quiz 3

1. expected returns, actual returns
2. risk aversion
3. risk neutral
4. risk takers
5. U.S. government securities
6. probability
7. probability distribution
8. expected rate of return
9. expected rate of return
10. probability distribution, risk

11. standard deviation, s
12. standard deviation, narrower, lower
13. $\sigma = \Sigma\ (K_i - K^{\wedge})^2 P_i$
14. variance
15. coefficient of variation
16. lower

Quiz 4

1. diversification, lowers
2. return, risk
3. expected return on a portfolio, a weighted average of all of the expected returns on each stock in a portfolio, or ($K^{\wedge}p = W_1K_1 + W_2K_2 + W_3K_3$)
4. portfolio risk
5. portfolio effect
6. correlation coefficient, r
7. low
8. Capital asset pricing model, CAPM
9. CAPM
10. risk-free rate
11. K_m
12. company-specific or unsystematic risk
13. beta coefficient, β
14. 1.0
15. beta, 1.0, riskier

16. market risk premium
17. security market line, SML
18. rate of inflation, changes in risk aversion

Quiz 5

1. stock
2. loan
3. par value
4. one thousand dollars
5. coupon interest rate, dividing
6. market interest
7. maturity date
8. an annuity
9. coupon payment paid each period(PVIFA) + (bond par value at maturity(PVIF))
10. market interest rate, number of periods remaining until maturity
11. decreases
12. discount
13. (old payment − new payment) × (PVIFA@new rate and periods)
14. premium
15. inverse, decrease
16. current yield
17. yield to maturity
18. n (time periods), PV (bond's current price), PMT (coupon

payment), FV (par value), then press i.

19. yield to call
20. there is no answer to this question
21. call premium
22. preferred stock
23. common stock
24. div/discount rate
25. $K_p = Div/PV$
26. capital gain
27. capital loss
28. Gordon growth model, $P_0 = D_1/(K_s - g)$
29. $D_1 = D_0(1 + g)$
30. market price, dividends
31. quickly, at a constant rate, slower
32. supernormal
33. the dividend, constant growth formula, PVIF, dividends, present value of the stock
34. our Standard Deviants insert cards
35. constant growth model, dividends, constant growth model

Quiz 6

1. raise capital (or money)
2. bonds
3. cost of capital
4. capital structure

ANSWERS

5. weighted average cost of capital, WACC
6. after-tax cost of debt
7. $K_d(1 - T)$
8. cost of preferred stock, D_{ps}/P_n
9. retained earnings
10. CAPM, bond-yield-risk premium approach, discounted cash flow
11. $K_s = K_{rf} + b(K_m - K_{rf})$
12. three to five percent, adjust for risk
13. stocks, retained earnings
14. discounted cash flow, DCF
15. $K_s = (div/price) + g$
16. flotation costs
17. $K_e = [div/price(1 - F)]\ 1g$
18. divide, stock price
19. $WACC = W_dK_d(1 - T) + W_{ps}K_{ps} + W_{ce}K_s$
20. cost of retained earnings
21. the cost of new common stock
22. marginal cost of capital
23. target capital structure
24. financial manager
25. increases

Quiz 7

1. capital budgeting
2. capital
3. capital investments
4. top executives
5. mandatory, expansion, replacement
6. mandatory
7. replacement
8. expansion projects
9. determine the cost of project, estimate expected cash flows project will create, estimate riskiness of the projected cash flows, determine the cost of capital at which the cash flows should be discounted, estimate revenues of the project using expected cash flows to calculate present value, compare the present value of the expected cash flows to the required outlay.
10. reject
11. payback, discounted payback, net present value, profitability index, internal rate of return, modified internal rate of return
12. payback or discounted payback
13. shorter, long, shorter
14. (unrecovered cash/break-even cash flow) 1 year b/f
15. $CF_0 + \frac{CF_1}{(1 + k)^1} + \frac{CF_2}{(1+k)^2} + \frac{CF_3}{(1+k)^3}$
16. it does not consider the time value of money, it ignores all cash flows beyond the payback period
17. subsequent cash flows

18. net present value
19. determine the present value of the cash flows, add the present value of the cash flows, subtract the initial investment
20. negative
21. profitability index
22. PV of cash inflows / cost of investment
23. present value of a project's expected cash flows, present value of the project's expected costs
24. cost of capital, cost of capital, more
25. internal rate of return (IRR)
26. modified internal rate of return (MIRR)
27. sum of the future values of a project's cash flows
28. greater
29. financial calculator
30. reinvested into the project

Quiz 8

1. cash flow
2. incremental cash flows
3. net investment cash outlay, operating cash flows,
4. net investment cash outlay, NICO
5. operating cash flows, OCFs, annual
6. revenue, operating expenses, depreciation, taxes, depreciation
7. net disposal cash flow

8. liquidation
9. removal
10. liquidation cash, removal costs, taxes, plus net working capital

Practice Exam 1

1. b

2. c

3. c

4. a

5. d

6. c

7. b

8. d

9. b
10. c

11. a

12. e

ANSWERS

13. c PVannuity = 325,000 × 10.5940 = $3,443,050

14. a FVannuity = 1,500 × 4.440 = $6,660

15. d FVannuity due = 1,500 × 4.440(1.07) = $7,126

16. b

17. a PVannuity = 500 × 11.4699 = $5,734.95

18. e PVannuity = 500 × (PVIFA [3%, 40])
= 500 × 23.1148
= $11,557.39

19. b

20. a

21. c

22. a. $PV = \frac{150{,}000}{0.05}$
$= \$3{,}000{,}000$

23. e. $EAR = \left(1+\frac{0.22}{12}\right)^{12} - 1$

$= 1.0183^{12} - 1$
$= 0.2436$

"There is no 'there' there."

Gertrude Stein

24. d. FV = (100)(1.311) + (300)(1.225) + (600)(1.145) + (900)(1.070) + 1200 = $3,348.60

25. b. $K^{\wedge} = (0.30)(0.15) + (0.50)(0.08) + (0.20)(0)$

$= 0.085$

$\cong 8.5\%$

26. c

27. a

28. b

29. a

30. First, calculate the beta of your current portfolio to determine your overall risk and a basis of comparison.

$\beta_p = W_1b_1 + W_2b_2 + W_3b_3$

$\beta_p = (0.40)(1.2) + (0.35)(0.85) + (0.25)(1.4)$

$= 1.1275$ current beta of your portfolio

β new portfolio $= (0.30)(1.2) + (0.35)(0.85) + (0.25)(1.4) + (0.10)(1.4)$

$= 1.1475$

Although it is only a slight increase, the overall beta of your portfolio would increase if stock D is added. Since you are

ANSWERS

extremely risk averse, you would not add the new stock. However, you could easily argue that not enough information is given to complete the problem, because even extremely risk averse investors would want to know what kind of return a new investment would provide. Even the most risk averse dork would accept a small fraction of risk for an enormous return.

31. You need to calculate the present value of the annuity compare it to the cash prize in present-day dollars.

    PVannuity = PAY (PVIFA)

    PVannuity = 60,000 (PVIFA [6%, 10pds])

    = 60,000 (7.3601)

    = $441,606

So, you would decide to take the $500,000 cash prize instead of the annuity which is only worth $441,606.

32. Use the CAPM formula to determine the required rate of return on Boogerglue's stock.

$$\text{CAPM} = K_{rf} + \beta(K_m - K_{rf})$$

$$= 7 + 1.9(10-7)$$

$$= 7 + 5.7$$

$$= 12.7\%$$

The required rate of return on Boogerglue's stock is 12.7% and you expect that you can receive a return of only 8%, so you would decide not to invest in Boogerglue.

33. First, set up a table with the information given.

Economy	Probability	Fishface
Boom	20	80
Normal	70	20
Recession	10	−15

Then, calculate the expected rate of return.

$$K\wedge = P_1(O_1) + P_2(O_2) + P_3(O_3)$$

$$= (0.20)(0.80) + (0.70)(0.20) + (0.10)(-0.15)$$

$$= (0.16) + (0.14) + (-.015)$$

$$= 0.285$$

$$= 28.5\% \text{ expected rate of return}$$

Then use that information to calculate the standard deviation:

$$\sigma = \Sigma(K_i - K\wedge)^2 P_i$$

To calculate the standard deviation, break it down into easy steps.

ANSWERS

First, take the expected rate of return (28.5%) and subtract it from each of the possible returns on Fishface's stock to get a set of deviations:

$$80 - 28.5 = 51.5$$
$$20 - 28.5 = -8.5$$
$$-15 - 28.5 = -43.5$$

Now, square each of these results:

$$(51.5)^2 = 2,652.25$$
$$(-8.5)^2 = 72.25$$
$$(-43.5)^2 = 1,892.25$$

Then multiply each of these results by the probability of each of the situations occurring and add them all together (this gives you the variance):

$$2,652.25\ (0.20) = 530.45$$
$$72.25\ (0.70) = 50.57$$
$$1,892.25\ (0.10) = \underline{189.23}$$
$$770.25 \text{ variance}$$

Take the square root of the variance to get the standard deviation:

$\sqrt{770.25} = 27.75\%$ standard deviation on Fishface stock

And, finally, the coefficient of variation:

$$CV = \frac{\sigma}{K^\wedge}$$

$$CV = \frac{27.75}{28.5}$$

$$= 0.97$$

34. Now, do the same for Dog Chew.

First make a table and calculate the expected rate of return on Dog Chew stock:

Economy	Probability	Dog Chew Return
Boom	20	70
Normal	70	30
Recession	10	5

$K^\wedge = (0.20)(0.70) + (0.70)(0.30) + (0.10)(0.05)$

$= (0.14) + (0.21) + (0.005)$

$= 0.355$

$= 35.5\%$ expected rate of return

ANSWERS

Now, we can use the two tables we've created to get the information we need to plot the two stocks on a probability distribution. So set up a graph, plot the points where the probability of the economic condition meets the expected return on the stock under that condition, and once you've plotted all three for each stock, connect the dots to get your distribution curve:

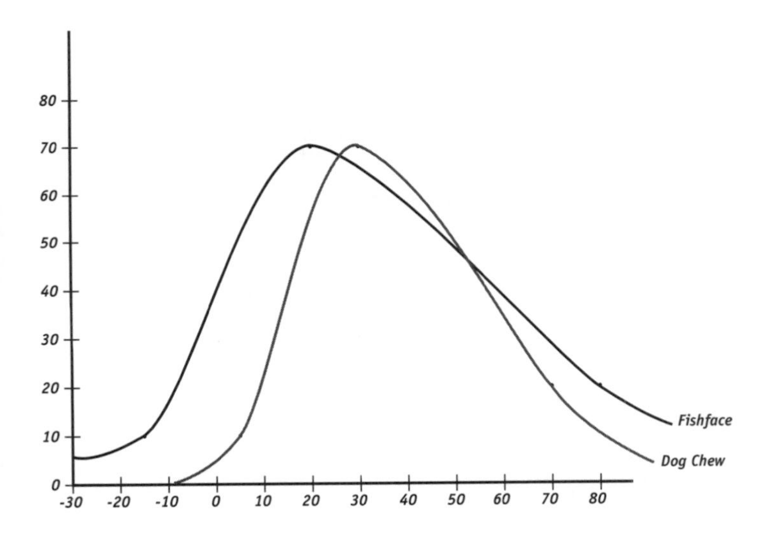

Then, look at the probability distributions of each stock and you can see that although they are close, Dog Chew has a more pointed distribution.

Therefore, if you are a risk averse investor, you would decide to invest in Dog Chew because the more pointed a probability distribution, the lower the risk of the security.

Practice Exam 2

1. c

2. b $FV = PV\,(FVIF\,[8\%, 4])$

$FV = 1{,}000(1.360)$

$FV = 1{,}360$

3. a $PVannuity = Pay(PVIFA\,[5\%, 20])$

$PVannuity = 500(12.4622)$

$= \$6{,}231.10$

4. a $PV = \frac{PAY}{i}$

$PV = \frac{200}{0.07}$

$PV = 2{,}857.14$

5. c Using the PVIFA and PVIF tables,

$BPV = \text{Coupon Payment (PVIFA)} + \text{Par Value (PVIF)}$

$= 60(8.5595) + 1000(0.3152)$

$= 828.77$

6. a No, because the present value is less than the price of $900.

ANSWERS

7. d 15-year maturity − 5 years = 10 years remaining

$$\begin{aligned} BPV &= 60(PVIFA\ [8\%, 10]) + 1000(PVIF\ [8\%, 10]) \\ &= 60(6.7101) + 1000(0.4632) \\ &= 865.80 \end{aligned}$$

8. c

9. d

10. b

11. a

$$\text{current yield} = \frac{\text{interest pay}}{\text{bond price}}$$

$$\text{current yield} = \frac{65}{875}$$

$$= 0.0743$$

$$\cong 7.43\%$$

12. a

13. c

14. d

$$K_p = \frac{\text{Div}}{\text{PV}}$$

$$K_p = \frac{50}{900}$$

$$= 0.0555$$

$$\cong 5.55\%$$

15. b $D_1 = D_0(1 + g)$

$= 4(1 + 0.10)$

$= 4.40$

$$= \frac{D_1}{K_s - g}$$

$$= \frac{4.40}{(0.12 - 0.10)}$$

$= 220$

16. a

17. a

18. b False. The correct steps are

1. Determine the PV of the dividends.

2. Apply the constant growth formula.

3. Discount the normal value to PV using the PVIF.

4. Discount dividends from supernormal periods and add them to PV of stock in step 3.

19. c after-tax cost of debt $= K_d(1 - T)$

$= 0.07(1 - .40)$

$= 0.042$

$\cong 4.2\%$

ANSWERS

20. d 5% underwriting charge ➡ \$7/share

net issuing price = \$140 − 7

= \$133

$$K_{ps} = \frac{D_{ps}}{P_p}$$

$$K_{ps} = \frac{12}{133}$$

= 0.090

≅ 9%

21. b

22. d $K_s = K_{rf} + \beta(K_m - K_{rf})$

$= 7 + 1.7(11 - 7)$

$= 13.8$

$\cong 13.8\%$

23. a $K_s = \dfrac{DIV_1}{Price} + g$

$= \dfrac{2}{47} + .075$

$= 0.1175$

$\cong 11.75\%$

24. b $K_e = \frac{Div}{Price}(1 - F) + g$

$$F = \frac{2.5}{47}$$

$$= 0.053$$

$$K_e = \frac{2.50}{47}(1 - 0.053) + 0.075$$

$$= 0.131167$$

$$= 13.12\%$$

25. c

26. e

27. b

28. d $NPV = \frac{CF_1}{(1+k)^1} + \frac{CF_2}{(1+k)^2} + \frac{CF_3}{(1+k)^3}$

$$= \frac{5{,}000}{(1+0.14)^1} + \frac{3{,}500}{(1+0.14)^2} + \frac{1{,}500}{(1+0.14)^3}$$

$$= 8091.59$$

$$NPV = \$8{,}091.59 - \$9{,}000 \text{ investment}$$

$$= -\$908.41$$

29. b

30. g

ANSWERS

31. Step 1:

Year 0 dividend = \$3.00

18% growth

Year 1 dividend = \$3.54

18% growth

Year 2 dividend = \$4.18

8% growth

Year 3 dividend = \$4.51

Step 2: Apply the constant growth formula.

$$= \frac{4.51}{(0.10 - 0.08)}$$

$$= \frac{4.51}{0.02}$$

$$= 225.50$$

Step 3:

$$PV = 225.50(PVIF\ [10\%,2])$$

$$= (225.50)(0.8264)$$

$$= 186.35$$

Step 4:

$$D_1 = 3.54\ (\text{PVIF}\ [10\%,1])$$
$$= 3.54\ (0.9091)$$
$$= \$3.22$$

$$D_2 = 4.18\ (\text{PVIF}\ [10\%,2])$$
$$= 4.18\ (0.8264)$$
$$= \$3.45$$

Then, add it all up.

$Div_1 =$ 3.22 PLUS

$Div_2 =$ 3.45 PLUS

Constant growth = <u>186.35</u>

= 193.02

The total PV of supernormal stock is $193.02.

32. Use a financial calculator:

Enter	−900	PV
Enter	90	PMT
Enter	5	n
Enter	1050	FV

(FV is par value of 1,000 plus 5% for the call premium.)

Press i and get YTC = 12.59

ANSWERS

33. $WACC = W_d K_d(1 - T) = W_{ps} K_{ps} + W_s K_s$

$WACC = (0.50)(8.4) + (0.10)(10.6) + (0.40)(13.75)$

$WACC = (4.2) + (1.06) + (5.5)$

$WACC = 10.76\%$

34. Use a financial calculator:

Enter	−9000	CF_0
Enter	5000	CF_1
Enter	3500	CF_2
Enter	1500	CF_3
Enter	850	CF_4

Press IRR and get 11.0133, then round down to 11% for your answer.

35. **NICO** = cost of equipment + change in net working capital
= 10,000 + 6,000
= $16,000

Net operating income = revenue − expenses
= 8,000 − 3,000
= 5,000 / year

Depreciation values

Year 1: 10,000(0.33) = 3,300

Year 2: 10,000(0.45) = 4,500

Year 3: 10,000(0.15) = 1,500

Earnings before taxes

Year 1: (5,000 − 3,300) = 1,700

Year 2: (5,000 − 4,500) = 500

Year 3: (5,000 − 1,500) = 3,500

Taxes per year

Year 1: 1,700 (0.25) = 425

Year 2: 500 (0.25) = 125

Year 3: 3,500 (0.25) = 875

Earnings after taxes

Year 1: (1,700 − 425)= 1,275

Year 2: (500 − 125) = 375

Year 3: (3,500 − 875)= 2,625

Add back depreciation to get operating cash flows:

Year 1 (1,275 + 3,300) = 4,575

Year 2 (375 + 4,500) = 4,875

Year 3 (2,625 + 1,500) = 4,125

ANSWERS

Determine book value of equipment after 3 years:

Depreciated 93% of value (33% + 45% + 15%)

7% is undepreciated

7% of $10,000 equipment = $700 book value

Determine capital gain/loss from sale of equipment at the end of year 3:

Sale price	600
Book value	700
Cap. G/L	−100
Taxes	0.25
	−25

Liquidation proceeds (sale price − taxes)

600 − (−25) = 625

Adjust year 3 cash flow to reflect the liquidation and return of net working capital:

Year 3 OCF = 4,125

Return of NWC	6,000
Proceeds of sale	+ 625
Adjusted CF	10,750

"If someone asks you if you're a god, you say YES."

Ghostbusters

So, the cash flows for the three-year life of the project are the following:

Year 0	−16,000
Year 1	4,575
Year 2	4,875
Year 3	10,750

Solution for Fina Crosso

PORTFOLIO
RISK
BLACKANDTAN
IRR
PREMIUM
STOCK
TOYS
TABIS
CAPITAL
ASSET
MIRR
INFLATION
TWIG

PERPETUITY
ERASECAR
CORPORATION
COMPOUNDING
LIABILITIES
BANKRUPTCY
KILN
YIELD
BET
DEBT
DEPRECIATION
ANNUITY
CAPM
DISCOUNT
BOND
COFFEE
TREASURER
SUSHI
INTEREST
GUM
ICING
WACC

Solution for FinoSearcho

Y	C	A	N	N	U	I	T	Y	O	G	O	H	R
T	O	I	T	S	E	R	E	T	N	I	K	E	H
I	R	D	N	E	D	I	V	I	D	Y	K	N	Y
L	P	E	T	U	S	T	D	L	T	O	O	S	T
I	O	T	A	I	E	N	T	I	R	I	A	I	Y
B	R	N	B	S	U	T	U	B	T	T	O	C	I
A	A	A	S	O	U	T	E	A	E	I	T	A	E
I	T	A	P	I	E	R	L	B	L	P	E	P	L
L	I	M	C	P	A	F	E	O	U	U	E	I	D
G	O	I	R	S	N	T	F	R	K	C	O	T	S
C	N	E	E	I	A	T	K	P	T	S	F	A	H
G	P	C	R	R	R	N	E	B	H	K	I	L	N
C	A	I	I	O	A	L	E	J	A	N	D	R	O
R	R	P	P	B	E	D	N	O	B	S	T	I	R

GLOSSARY

accounting equation — Assets are equal to liabilities plus capital or owners' equity.

after-tax cost of debt [$K_d(1 - T)$] — Market interest rate of the debt, minus the tax savings that result because the interest is tax deductible. Used to calculate the WACC.

agency problem (stockholder-bondholder) — Conflicts of interest between stockholders and bondholders with regard to risk.

agency problem (stockholder-manager) — Conflicts between the interests of stockholders, and the managers who run the day-to-day operations. When this condition arises, managers focus on maximizing their personal wealth and not that of the shareholders.

amortized loan — Series of equal payments over time that include the payment of interest on the principal. Amortized loans are reported on an amortization schedule, where the principal balance is reduced to zero at maturity.

annual percentage rate (APR) — An interest rate term. The periodic rate multiplied by the number of compounding periods.

annual report — The most important report that the financial manager produces. Prepared and issued annually by a corporation to its stockholders. Includes all of the company's yearly audited financial information as well as commentary by the officers of the organization.

annuity due — Rare annuity whose payments are made at the beginning of the period.

annuity — Stream of equal payments made over a certain time period at fixed intervals.

asset — Something of value that may provide future or present benefit.

balance sheet — One of the reports in a corporation's annual report. It provides a glimpse of a business's financial position at a specific time.

bankruptcy — Point at which a firm or other entity is unable to honor its financial commitments. One or more claimants (people owed money) can go to the bankruptcy courts to seek appropriate compensation. Bankruptcy can be resolved by either giving the firm more time to honor debts, or selling all or part of the business to pay off the creditors.

Beta (β) — A measure of the tendency of a stock's return to move with the market's general return. Measures the volatility of an individual security relative to the entire market.

beta of the portfolio — Weighted average of the betas of all stocks in a given portfolio.

Glossary

bond — Long-term debt instrument issued by a business or government. The purchaser (lender) either receives a series of interest payments over time or a discount on the par value.

bond present value (BPV) — Equals the total coupon payment paid each period on a bond, multiplied by the PVIFA, plus the bond par value at maturity times the PVIF.

bond-yield-plus-risk-premium approach — A method used to determine the cost of retained earnings. Based on the theory that businesses with risky, high-interest rate debt will also have risky, high-cost equity. The process of taking a company's interest rate on its long-term debt and adding three to five percentage points to it to adjust for risk, then using that figure as the company's cost of retained earnings.

break-even point — Point at which the total costs of a project equal the total revenues generated by a project.

broker — Someone who buys and/or sells securities on behalf of others.

call premium — Amount above a bond's par value that a company agrees to pay the investor for exercising call provisions included in the bond's indenture.

capital — Money used to finance a business's operations.

capital asset pricing model (CAPM) — Determines the relationship between risk and return on stocks held in the market portfolio and helps investors to decide what risks they are willing to take on particular investments while taking into consida-

tion the investment's rate of return. Based on the theory that any stock's required rate of return equals the risk-free rate of return, plus a risk premium that reflects only the risk remaining after diversification. Method used to determine the cost of retained earnings.

capital budgeting — Process of analyzing investment prospects and making long-term investment decisions based on that analysis.

capital component — Any one of the types of capital that businesses use to raise money: debt, preferred stock, retained earnings, new common stock.

capital investments — Very large, long-term investments that require large sums of capital. They may dramatically affect the direction and success of a business (i.e., investment in new equipment, new product development, or the acquisition of another business).

capital markets — Financial markets for investments with a term of one year or longer, such as stocks and long-term debt.

capital structure — Way that a company organizes capital components to raise capital (money).

cash flow — Accounting of the hard cash that comes in and out of a company.

chief financial officer (CFO) — Person responsible for the financial management of a corporation.

Glossary

coefficient of variation — Standardized measure of the risk per unit of return for single stock investments. Calculated as the expected standard deviation divided by the expected rate of return. Also referred to as the risk return trade-off.

coelon — Product of Vermont. Friend of Igor. All-around keen.

common equity — Common stock and retained earnings.

common stock — Ownership interest in a business. Entitles its owner to dividends (if the business has sufficient earnings) and full voting rights.

common stockholder's equity — In an accounting sense, a company's assets minus its liabilities, minus its preferred stock. Also referred to as the corporation's net worth.

company-specific risk — Risk that a company incurs in its day-to-day operations.

compounding — Process of adding interest to an existing balance (the principal) at regular intervals. Occurs when interest is added to existing interest.

compounding period — Period over which the compounding of interest takes place.

comptroller — Corporate manager responsible for performing hands-on financial work, such as accounting, payroll, and taxes.

constant growth or normal growth — Growth that is expected to continue into the foreseeable future at about the same rate as

the economy as a whole. Constant growth stocks are more valuable than non-growth stocks.

constant growth model or Gordon growth model — Used to find the value of a constant growth stock. Uses present value and dividends to determine a fair price for common stock.

corporate income tax — Income tax paid by corporations. The government taxes corporations separately, which results in double taxation on dividend income.

corporation — A legal entity created by the government as a separate legal body for the explicit purpose of conducting business. Corporations have unlimited life, easy transferability of ownership, and limited liability.

correlation coefficient — Statistical measurement that signifies the tendency of two securities to move together. Can range from +1.0 to -1.0.

cost of capital — Percentage that represents how much of every dollar was spent in the process of getting that same dollar. A financial concept used to determine how much money must be spent to make even more money.

cost of issuing new common stock (K_e) — Cost of retained earnings plus flotation costs. Equal to the expected dividend divided by the stock price, times one minus the percentage flotation cost, plus growth.

Glossary

cost of preferred stock (K_{ps}) — Rate of return that investors require on a company's preferred stock. Equal to the dividend divided by the net issuing price.

cost of retained earnings — Rate of return the stockholders require on the business. Can be calculated using one of three methods: CAPM, the bond-yield-plus-risk-premium approach, or the discounted cash flow approach.

coupon interest rate — Annual interest rate on a bond. Can be calculated by dividing the coupon payment by the par value.

coupon payment — Number of dollars of interest paid on a bond each period. Coupon payments typically occur every six months.

current yield - Annual interest payment on a bond divided by the bond's current price.

debt — Fixed obligations to repay borrowed funds.

deferred annuity — Another name for an ordinary annuity in which the payment occurs at the end of the period.

depreciation — Charge for assets used in production. Not an actual cash outlay. Annual charge against a business' income which reflects the dollar cost of the equipment used up in the production process.

depreciation benefit — Amount that a new piece of equipment depreciates over and above the amount that the equipment being replaced depreciates. Used to calculate the tax savings from depreciation.

discount bond — Bond that sells below its par value because the market interest rate is greater than the bond's coupon rate.

discounted cash flow approach (DCA) — Method used to determine the cost of retained earnings. Based on the theory that if a stock is growing at a steady rate, the required rate of return will equal the company's bond yield plus the growth rate.

discounted payback method — Method used to determine whether to accept a capital project. A variation of the payback method. Adjusts a capital project's revenues by the cost of capital, thereby accounting for the time value of money.

discounting — Calculating the present value by accounting for the time value of money.

discount rate — Percentage involving money that investors do not get to keep.

diversification — Investment in a broad range of securities to reduce risk. Typically includes investing in companies in various industries.

dividend — Cash distribution paid to shareholders. The periodic return on stocks to the investor.

GLOSSARY

dividend policy — Corporate policy that determines how much of a firm's net income is held in retained earnings and how much is paid out to shareholders as dividends. An important policy for the financial manager to develop and maintain to increase the entire worth of the business.

earnings per share — Net income created by a corporation's operations, divided by the number of shares of common stock outstanding. Important to the determination of stock price.

effective annual rate (EAR) — The true annual rate of interest that is earned or charged, as opposed to the quoted rate. It includes the compounding of interest.

erasecar — Small rubber racer.

expansion project — Type of capital project. Investment made by a business to move into a new market or expand within an existing market. Intended to increase sales.

expected rate of return (K^) — Rate of return an investor expects to receive from an investment. Technically, it represents the weighted average of returns over different states of the economy.

expected return on a portfolio — Weighted average of all expected returns on each individual component, or security, held in the portfolio.

externalities — Effects of a capital project on the cash flows of other parts of the business.

financial manager — Corporate manager responsible for obtaining and using funds to maximize the entire worth of the business. The financial manager's primary goal is to maximize stockholder wealth.

fixed costs — Costs such as rent and equipment, which do not change with a change in output.

flotation cost — Percentage cost of issuing new common stock. All of the expenses incurred through the issuing of new stock.

forecasting — Estimating the future financial condition of a business. Usually based on recent trends of the business plus prospects for the nation's or region's economy.

future value — Amount that a present sum of money will grow to in the future when compounded by an interest rate.

future value interest factor (FVIF) — Future value of one dollar after *n* periods at the rate of i per period. Can be determined by using a FVIF table if the interest rate and number of periods are known.

general partnership — Type of business organization in which each partner is involved in the day-to-day management and has unlimited liability for the debts the business incurs.

golden parachute — Large bonus paid to outgoing executives during corporate buyouts.

Gordon growth model — See constant growth model.

growth cycles — Cycles that companies typically go through during their lives. The companies grow quickly early in their life spans, then they grow at a constant rate, and finally, toward the end of their life span, their growth is slower than that of the economy.

hostile takeover — Unwanted buyout bid by another corporation, individual, or group despite the opposition of the corporation's existing management. The threat of such a takeover typically motivates managers to act in the best interests of stockholders and focus on increasing earnings per share.

icing — Hockey violation that causes a faceoff in the violator's defensive zone. Icing occurs when an offensive player propels the puck from behind the centerline to a point behind the goal, without any intervening offensive player touching the puck. Icing is canceled, or waved off, if the puck passes through the crease or could have been touched by a defensive player before the puck passed the back red line.

income statement — Financial statement summarizing a company's earnings and its expenses over a period of time (usually one year).

incremental cash flow — Cash flows directly related to a particular project. Analyzed to determine the difference that the cash flows generated by a project make in a business's operations.

indenture — Written agreement or contract that the business or government issuing a bond provides to the investor. Details the amount borrowed and promises to repay that amount plus a specific amount of interest over a certain period.

inflation — Tendency of prices to increase over time.

inflation premium (IP) — Premium for expected inflation included in the real risk-free rate of return.

interest rate — Amount paid for use of borrowed capital. Fee a lender charges for use of its money. Percentage that includes money the investor gets to keep.

"Depressing teenagers is like shooting fish in a barrel."

The Simpsons

internal rate of return (IRR) — Method used to determine whether to accept a capital project. Process of calculating the discount rate that forces the present value of the capital project's expected cash flows to equal the present value of the project's expected costs. Once calculated, the IRR is compared to the project's cost of capital. If a capital project's IRR is greater than the cost of capital, the project will be profitable, and therefore accepted. Assumes that the revenue generated by the project is being reinvested in the project. Method business executives prefer.

investment banker — Agent who acts as the middleman, finding firms that need funds and matching them up with firms or investors willing to invest funds.

kiln — Oven for baking ceramics.

GLOSSARY

liabilities — Claims against a company's assets. Current liabilities include accounts payable and long-term liabilities include long-term debt.

limited partnership — Type of business organization that includes both general and limited partners. The limited partner supplies capital and is liable only for the amount of his or her investment. General partners supply expertise and run the day-to-day operations of the business.

liquidating — Process of turning an asset into cash.

mandatory project — Type of capital project. Required by some entity other than the business itself (like the government or a union). Also called safety projects because they typically relate to safety.

marginal cost of capital — Cost of obtaining one more dollar of new capital.

market interest rate — Rate of interest offered on new bonds today. Fluctuates daily.

market risk or systematic risk — Portion of a security's risk that cannot be eliminated through diversification. Common to all securities. May also be referred to as relevant risk.

market risk premium — Compensates for assuming an average amount of risk. Additional return over the risk-free rate required by investors. Expected rate of return on the market minus the risk-free rate.

maturity date — Specified date on which the par value of a bond must be repaid.

modified accelerated cost recovery system (MACRS) — Federal government guidelines for depreciation. Chart that consists of a series of depreciation lengths, or classes, based on the durability of the depreciable item and its expected life span.

modified internal rate of return (MIRR) — Method used to determine whether to accept a capital project. Process of calculating the discount rate that forces the present value of the project's cost of capital to equal the present value of its terminal value. Assumes that the revenue generated by a capital project is being reinvested in the business but not necessarily in the project. Once calculated, the MIRR is compared to the project's cost of capital. If a capital project's MIRR is greater than its cost of capital, the project will be profitable, and therefore, accepted.

money markets — Short-term financial markets in which money is borrowed for less than one year.

mortgages — Loans on real estate.

net disposal cash flow — Type of cash flow generated by a business evaluating a capital investment. Final cash flow resulting from ending a project. Cash inflow. Equals the liquidation cash, minus any removal costs, minus income taxes, plus any net working capital caught up in the project.

net investment cash outlay (NICO) — Type of cash flow generated by a business evaluating a capital investment. All of the money required to start a particular capital project. Cash out-

flow needed to purchase new equipment plus any changes to the business's net working capital required to begin a new project.

net present value method (NPV) — Method used to determine whether to accept a capital project. An accounting of the capital project's benefits, versus its costs, accounting for the time value of money. Discounts the project's revenues using the present value formula, then adds all the revenues to the project's investment to determine whether the project makes or loses money.

operating cash flows (OCFs) — Type of cash flow generated by a business evaluating a capital investment. The change in a business's cash flows that is a direct result of a particular capital project. Money that a business is actually bringing in from a capital project. Calculated annually. Total income from a project minus its total costs, minus its depreciation, minus the taxes, then plus the depreciation.

opportunity cost rate — Expected rate of return for an alternative investment of similar risk.

par value — Face-value of a bond. Amount of money that the business or government borrows and promises to repay at a specific date in the future. Typically $1,000.

payback method — Method used to determine whether to accept a capital project. The first method ever used in capital budgeting decisions. Calculates the number of years required for a capital project to break even.

periodic rate — Interest rate a lender charges or a borrower pays per compounding period.

perpetuity — Annuity with a never-ending, constant stream of fixed payments.

portfolio — Investor's assortment of securities.

portfolio risk — Risk involved in investing in a group of securities.

preferred stock — Combination of common stock and bonds. Stock that has fixed dividend payments but does not grant voting rights to its holder. A preferred stockholder must be paid dividends before common stockholders but need not be paid before bondholders.

premium bond — Bond that sells for a price above its par value because the market interest rate falls below the bond's coupon rate.

present value (PV) — Today's value of money, to be received in the future.

present value interest factor (PVIF) — Present value of one dollar due *n* periods in the future discounted at i percent per period. Can be determined by using a PVIF table if the interest rate and number of periods is known.

president or chief executive officer (CEO) — Person responsible for the management of a corporation. Reports to the corporation's board of directors.

Glossary

primary market — Financial market in which newly issued securities are bought and sold.

principal — Amount of money initially borrowed or invested.

probability — Likelihood of achieving a specific outcome. Chance.

probability distribution — Listing of all possible outcomes or events. A probability is assigned to each outcome.

profitability index method (PI) — Method used to determine whether to accept a capital project. Used to compare projects of different sizes by comparing the present values of their cash flows.

proxy fight — Method used to address agency problems; the board of directors presents the stockholders with the problem and they vote whether or not to remove the manager in question from office.

rate of return — Amount of money an investor earns on an investment.

quoted or nominal rate — Interest rate that is stated by lenders or borrowers.

real rate (K*) — Interest rate on a riskless security if no inflation is present. Expected rate of return on a financial investment after subtracting the risk premium and inflation premium.

removal costs — Costs incurred in the process of liquidating an asset or project.

STUDY SIDEKICK

replacement project — Type of capital project. Investment a business makes to replace old, damaged, or obsolete equipment.

required rate of return — Minimum rate of return on a financial instrument that an investor will accept.

retained earnings — Portion of a business' earnings that has been saved rather than paid out as dividends.

"Sometimes you kick, sometimes you get kicked."

INXS

risk — Difference between the expected and the actual. Probability of earning a return that differs from what was expected.

risk aversion — Term used to describe an investor's low tolerance for risk. Risk averse investors require higher rates of return on higher risk securities.

risk-free rate (K_{rf}) — Real rate of return plus the inflation premium. Equals the interest rate on U.S. Treasury securities.

risk neutral — The condition of being indifferent to risk.

risk premium — Difference between the expected rate of return on a risky security and a less risky security. Added to the inflation premium and the real rate of return to compensate for the risk of investing in a security.

risk takers — Investors who enjoy taking risks and prefer more risk to less.

secondary market — Financial market in which previously owned securities are bought and sold (i.e. the NYSE).

Glossary

security market line (SML) — Graphical depiction of the relationship between risk and the required rate of return for individual securities. Using the CAPM formula, the SML can graph a risk/return trade-off line for investors who invest in well-diversified portfolios.

sole proprietorship — Type of business organization owned by one person. The owner has unlimited liability for the organization, and is taxed only at the personal income level.

Standard Deviants — A registered trademark of Cerebellum Corporation.

standard deviation (s) — Statistical measurement of risk. Measures the difference between the expected rate of return and the actual rate of return. Measures the variability of a probability distribution.

statement of cash flows — Financial statement in the annual report that reports the impact of a business's operating, investing, and financing on cash flows over a period.

statement of retained earnings — Financial statement in the annual report that reports how much of the business's earnings were retained for investments in new projects.

stock — Security that pays a dividend and gives its holder partial ownership in a business.

stock options — Option to purchase stock at a prearranged price over a certain period of time. Usually given to managers to motivate them to increase the value of the company's stock.

supernormal or nonconstant growth — Portion of a company's life cycle in which its growth is much faster than that of the whole economy. Typically occurs at the beginning of a company's life cycle and is not sustainable.

swiss chard — Beet with nutritive leaves, which are often boiled.

systematic risk — See market risk.

tabis — Small monkeylike spirit with bat wings and venomous claws.

T-account — Accounting equation on which all financial statements are based. States that assets are equal to liabilities plus capital or owners' equity.

tender offer — Formal offer to purchase a controlling interest of the shares of a corporation at a price higher than market price.

terminal value — Sum of future values of a project's cash flows.

term structure of interest rates — Relationship between long- and short-term interest rates.

time value of money — The concept that the value of money changes over time.

GLOSSARY

treasurer — Person responsible for the management of a corporation's cash and investments, including the determination of how much debt and equity the business uses.

treasury bill — Short-term U.S. government security that matures in one year or less from the date of issue.

treasury bond — Long-term U.S. government security that matures in ten to thirty years from the date of issue.

treasury note — Long-term U.S. government security that matures in one to ten years from the date of issue.

underwriting cost — Cost of hiring someone to do all the work of issuing new stock.

unsystematic risk — See company-specific risk.

valuation — Process of appraising or estimating the worth of a financial security. Process investors use to determine whether an investment is profitable.

variable costs — Business costs that fluctuate, such as salaries.

variance —Square of the standard deviation.

weighted average cost of capital (WACC) — A weighted average cost of using all of the capital components (debt, preferred stock, and common equity) together.

writer — One of the various species of self-abusive primates.

yield — Actual return on a security.

yield curve — Graphical depiction of the relationship between yields and maturities of securities. A normal yield curve is upward sloping.

yield to call — Rate of return earned on a bond if it is called prior to its maturity date.

yield to maturity — The rate of return earned on a bond if it is held to maturity. Fluctuates with changes in bond prices.

zero growth stock — Common stock whose future dividends are not expected to grow.

Notes

STUDY SIDEKICK

"Your hair hangs like flax on a distaff; and I hope to see a housewife take thee between her legs and spin it off."

Twelfth Night

NOTES

Study Sidekick

NOTES

"Four of his five wits went halting off, and now he is the whole man governed with one."

Much Ado About Nothing

STUDY SIDEKICK

NOTES

THE
STANDARD
DEVIANTS

NOTES

STUDY SIDEKICK

NOTES

Study Sidekick

NOTES

Notes

Study Sidekick

Notes

Study Sidekick